CUT-OUTS AND CUT-UPS

COMING OUT!

MORE Lesbian Fun'n'Games

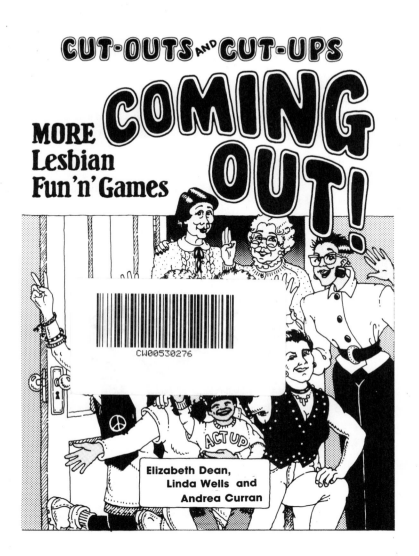

Elizabeth Dean,
Linda Wells and
Andrea Curran

With Illustrations by Ginger Brown

New Victoria Publishers Inc.

Published by New Victoria Publishers Inc., a feminist literary and cultural organization, PO Box 27 Norwich, Vermont 05055

Cover Design and illustrations by Ginger Brown
Additional material by Claudia Lamperti, Beth Dingman and Claire Smith

Some illustration material is from various Dover publications
Printed on recycled paper.

Disclaimer

The characters portrayed in this book, while they may greatly resemble your current lover, a roommate, the pitcher on your softball team, an ex-lover, or any member of the lesbian community, are fictitious. Any resemblance to a living or deceased person, or to a person you would like to be either living or deceased, is purely coincidental.

Acknowledgements

We would like to acknowledge the fact that many lesbians recognized that the first *Cut-outs and Cut-ups* was not a self-help book. In keeping with this tradition, please disregard anything that could be misconstrued as therapeutic advice in this book.

ISBN 0-934678-33-2

Library of Congress Cataloging-in-Publication Data

Wells, Linda.
    Coming out : more lesbian fun 'n games / Elizabeth Dean, Linda
Wells, and Andrea Curran.
        p.   cm.
    ISBN (invalid) 0-09-367833-2
    1. Lesbianism--Miscellanea. 2. Lesbians--Miscellanea.   I. Wells,
Linda. II. Curran, Andrea. III. Title.
HQ75.5.W45   1992
306.76'63--dc20   91-32875
                                                                      CIP

Elizabeth Dean dedicates this book to Linda and Andy, who always make her laugh.

Linda Wells would like to dedicate this book to two very important females in her life: Maude, for 10 years of unconditional love and cold-nose snuggles, and Susan for two years of the same.

Andrea Curran dedicates this book to Bonnie.

Introduction

In this sequel to *Cut-Outs and Cut-Ups: A Lesbian Fun 'n' Games Book*, we have tried to continue with a spirit of fun and gaiety (pun intended). Our new book, however, has an air of maturity about it (as proof, we rejected *Revenge of Cut-Outs and Cut-Ups* and *Daughter of Cut-Outs and Cut-Ups* as titles) and attempts to represent the optimistic integration of lesbians with society as a whole.

Once again, we have tried to be fair and offend everyone equally: execudykes, lesbian mothers, and S/M dykes alike (although we harbor a slight fear that we will be attacked by hoards of leather-clad motorcycle-riding lesbians wielding briefcases and dirty diapers). We have new and improved puzzles and games for you, as well as sophisticated literary references.

Mostly, we hope that you'll have fun with our new book; that you'll do the puzzles, play with the paper dolls, and maybe see aspects of yourself that you can laugh about. We also hope you'll tell all your friends to rush out and buy the book—we could use the money.

Table of Contents

WHAT YOUR DREAMS MEAN

Renowned feminist astrologer Imogene Carlotta Stars, or I. C. Stars as she is known to the faithful who have followed her for centuries throughout her (and their) past lives, has awakened the psychic world with her latest book, *LESBIAN DREAMS: What Goes On When the Lights Go Off.* She is the only astrologer to interpret the dreams of the lesbian population and to connect them with the lesbian world, not the straight world (where, as we all know, everything is viewed as a phallic symbol or a desire for heterosexual sex).

Ms. Star comments, "Dr. Sigmund Freud said that sometimes a cigar was just a cigar. I go one step further in my book. I ask: 'What if a lesbian dreams about a cigar? Why would she dream about it? Is the cigar an extension of that lesbian's life? If so, how? Is the cigar a smoke-screen for a deep, underlying issue in her life, or is it merely a stinking, filthy pile of tobacco leaves?' This is what today's lesbian wants to know!"

Here are excerpts from her latest work on interpreting common symbols often visualized by lesbians in their dreams.

Acorns

A symbol of lesbian love.

If you're gathering acorns in your dream—you want to meet as many women as possible.

If you're burying an acorn or some acorns—you want to hide an attraction to another woman or other women.

If a woman offers you acorns—she's nuts about you.

Airplanes

Airplane dreams often indicate unresolved softball fears.

If you dream your plane crashes—you fear being unable to score the winning run.

If you dream of a delayed takeoff—you fear that rain will cancel a tournament game.

If you dream of a rough landing in an airplane—you fear possible "cleat failure" while sliding into a base.

If you dream of taking off in an airplane—you fear being unable to hit anything but high, fly balls, easily catchable by the opposition.

What Your Dreams Mean

If you dream of throwing up in an airplane—you fear you'll strike out in front of your lover.

Bananas

Banana dreams are not phallic; rather, they merely indicate a low potassium level. So have a sliced banana on your cereal in the morning, and don't think anymore about it.

Bar

Dreaming about a bar indicates a desire to own a business that will attract lots of lesbians.

If you dream of drinking alone in a bar—you're afraid your business will fail.

If you dream of finding money on the floor of the bar, but the money has your father's face printed on the bill—you fear having to ask your father to co-sign a bank loan for a bar named *My Daughter Is a Lesbian.*

If you dream of trying to order one measly, watered-down drink in a crowded, smoke-filled bar as you're pressed against the dirty, sticky counter in the crush of a loud, obnoxious crowd where you can't even hold a decent conversation because the noise decibel level rivals a jumbo jet taking off six feet from you—your business will be successful, it will be franchised coast to coast, and you'll never have to spend another Saturday night alone again.

Bees

Dreaming about one bee indicates a fear of running into an ex-lover; dreaming about a hive of bees indicates a fear of running into all your ex-lovers at the same time.

Bondage

A dream in which your hands and/or feet are tied up or restricted in some way and in which you are lying, helpless and spread-eagle, on a bed has nothing whatsoever to do with sexual desire or a possible interest in S/M. Rather, the dream is a psychological indication of your need for more sleep; hence, you see yourself tied down in a bed and unable to get up.

Breasts

Breast dreams, like banana dreams, are nutritionally based and indicate your body's need for calcium. The larger the breasts are that you dream of, the greater your need for calcium.

Cats

The lesbian population is particularly susceptible to cat-anxiety dreams, possibly because they own 99.9% of all the domestic cats in the United States.

If you dream of being held captive and tortured by your cat—it's most likely time to change the kitty litter.

If you dream of a long-haired cat—it's time to trim your pubic hair.

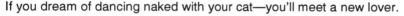

If you dream of dancing naked with your cat—you'll meet a new lover.

If you dream of your cat becoming Garfield—you desire lots of money.

If you dream of being suffocated by a cat while you're sleeping in a crib—your cat is probably playing with your "dream channel." Kick your cat off the bed, roll over, and go back to sleep.

Cigars

Lesbians who work in the corporate world often suffer from cigar dreams, particularly during times when they're up for a job promotion, raise, or job review. Cigar dreams are symbolically related to the desire to get ahead in the old-boy network and to try to fit in with back-slapping, pompous, conservative camaraderie of macho executives who, by their birth certificates, are old enough to drive, yet emotionally are stuck in their early teenage years.

If you dream of chomping on and/or spitting out a cigar—you want to bite the head off anyone who tries to step in your way up the corporate ladder, including your boss.

If you dream of slowly removing the paper band from a long, sleek, expensive cigar—you want to undress, and then sleep with, your attractive female boss.

If you dream of puffing rapidly on a cigar so you fill a room

What Your Dreams Mean

with clouds of foul-smelling smoke—you desire a corner office with a window.

If you dream of clenching a cigar between your teeth while you deliver your department's quarterly report—you have a hidden desire to be regarded as a meansonofabitch who can handle anything (even though you were reduced to tears when you saw a Liquid Paper smudge on your final report during your last PMS-stress time).

If you dream of handing cigars out to others—you may be hearing your biological clock tick away and could be considering juggling your career with motherhood.

Cows

Lesbians who dream of cows secretly wish one of two things: (1) that they could afford a black leather jacket, or (2) that they could eat a juicy hamburger without feeling politically incorrect.

Cucumbers and Other Vegetables

Dreams that involve cucumbers, zucchini, carrots, and other vegetables are not phallically based. Rather, lesbians who live off the land often dream about cucumbers and other vegetables when the multitude of seeds they planted in the spring are ready to be harvested. A vegetable-based dream is interpreted as part of a fantasy

that land-loving lesbians have after the initial "fun" of owning their farm wears off (which occurs sometime during the first year's harvest). The fantasy involves a telephone call or letter from a national grocery store chain that states it wishes to purchase, at top dollar, hundred of jars of pickled and preserved vegetables the lesbians put up every year and which, in total, could feed the entire continent of Africa for a decade.

Dentist

Being in a dentist's chair symbolizes a fear of having oral sex. However, being in a dentist's chair with someone means just the opposite.

4

What Your Dreams Mean

Dildo
Come on! What do you think dreaming about a dildo means?

Dogs
Dogs are symbols of protection and happiness for lesbians who are able to hike, camp, and run—while accompanied by these furry friends—with a certain sense of security. The bigger the dog is in your dream, the greater the sense of protection you feel in your life.

Eating (food) in Bed
This dream reflects your fantasy to own and operate a bed and breakfast inn. Eating something outside of the four major food groups reflects your desire for pleasure, not business.

Earthquake
Earthquake dreams denote a desire to stay as far away from San Francisco as possible, even if it is a famed lesbian mecca.

Fairy
Dreaming of a fairy means you secretly wish to be a gay male.

Flying
Dreaming that you are flying means you haven't fully accepted the theory that Amelia Earhart's plane simply ran out of gas and crashed.

Gymnasium
Dreaming of a gymnasium means you're thinking about the first gym teacher you ever had a crush on.

Hammer
Hammer dreams are often symbolic of great therapeutic breakthroughs, particularly when you dream that you hit a nail right on the head. But if you hit your thumb with the hammer, you can count on several more months of intensive therapy.

Handcuffs
If you dream of being handcuffed to another woman who playfully giggles and swallows the key, it's a sure sign that you're in for some difficult times.

What Your Dreams Mean

Jerks (as people, not verbs)

Dreams of people who are jerks symbolize the homophobic people in your life. If you kill one or more of the jerks in your dream, this is known as a "jerking off" dream.

Making love with famous women

Lesbians often dream of making love with famous women as a way of resolving their fantasies about lovers they would like to have in real life. Some of the more common women dreamed of are:

Bea Arthur, as the character of Maude—who symbolizes your desire to be with a loud, dominant, overbearing partner.

Lauren Bacall, in her heyday—who symbolizes your desire to be with a dame who you can treat like a dame.

Barbara Billingsley, as Mrs. Cleaver —who symbolizes the lesbian Oedipal Complex to kill your father and sleep with your ideal of a mother.

Jane Fonda—who symbolizes your desire to be with someone who will give you a good workout.

Shirley MacLaine—who symbolizes your desire to be with a woman who you may have known before.

Madonna—who symbolizes your desire to be a Wanna Be.

Mary Tyler Moore, as Laura Petrie—who symbolizes your desire to be with the "perfect" wife.

Nancy Reagan—who symbolizes your desire to be with a woman who says no to drugs, but yes to astrology.

Joan Rivers—who symbolizes your desire to be with a woman who will talk to you (and talk and talk and...)

Sigourney Weaver, in *Alien* and *Aliens* —who symbolizes your desire to be with someone who looks fresh and seductive in a panty/tank top combo when she hasn't showered, eaten, slept, or had a breath of fresh air in weeks.

Kate and Allie or Cagney and Lacey—who symbolize your desire to participate in a menage â trois with two gorgeous babes.

Motorcycle

A motorcycle dream is the lesbian version of the straight women's horseback riding dream. A motorcycle dream is purely sexual and symbolizes your desire to have something alive and vibrant between your legs.

What Your Dreams Mean

Nakedness

Any time you're naked in a dream, this expresses your fear of coming out.

Noah's Ark

Any dream about Noah's Ark reflects your vision of a lesbian Utopia in which only female creatures are paired together.

Nuked whales (or other endangered species)

When you dream of nuked whales or other endangered species, you can bet you've been spending too many hours working for causes.

Nuns

Dreaming of nuns symbolizes your desire to break old habits.

Orgasm

Dreaming that you're having an orgasm is one of those dreams everyone wants to have. So relax and enjoy it. But if you actually orgasm while you're dreaming, then you may be onto something. Don't bother getting out of bed. Just keep dreaming.

Pierced body parts

Dreams of pierced body parts are a sign of guilt.

If you dream of pierced ears—you don't feel good about the amount of money you spend annually on earrings to fill your six holes per ear.

If you dream of pierced genitals—you haven't dealt with your guilt about being a Catholic lesbian.

If you dream of a pierced nose—you're afraid to admit that you're bullish on Merrill Lynch.

What Your Dreams Mean

Pigs

Pigs in dreams foretell an invitation you'll receive to a pot-luck event.

Playing pool

Dreams of playing pool are about death and mortality; they express your fear that your tombstone will consist of a chalkboard that will show your first name, with a line drawn through it.

Quails

If you dream of quails, you're probably very concerned about the future of America.

Quicksand

Quicksand dreams symbolize networking in the women's community.

If you dream that you walk around a pit of quicksand—you have many valuable contacts who support you.

If you dream that you're sinking rapidly in quicksand—you need to find a better network—and fast!

Rabbits

Dreams about rabbits symbolize your fear that friends will discover you subscribe to *Playboy* magazine.

Sex toys

Dreams of sex toys have nothing at all to do with sex; rather, they symbolize your inability to come to terms with a childhood that was devoid of stuffed animals, board games, and a Lincoln Logs set.

Shoes

To dream of shoes is a sign that you'll be making a journey.

If you dream of wearing Birkenstock sandals—you'll be attending a women's music festival.

If you dream of wearing high heels—you'll be heading for a Tina Turner concert.

If you dream of wearing high tops—you'll be going to play in the N.B.A. (it's fan--tastic!).

If you dream of hiking boots—you'll be walking the Appalachian trail.

What Your Dreams Mean

If you dream of penny loafers—you'll go on a trip to look up an old lover.

If you dream of wearing sneakers—you'll be walking up and down Commercial Street in P-town.

If you dream of wearing no shoes—you'll be hopping into another woman's bed.

Softball

Dreams of playing softball means you secretly desire playing the field for awhile.

Tampons/sanitary napkins

When you dream of feminine hygiene products, your unconscious mind is trying to alert you to the fact that you've been caught unawares in the middle of the night.

Tattoo

Dreams of tattoos reflect your desire to become a colorful personality.

Therapist

Dreaming about your therapist ex-presses an anxiety about money; you may be worried about how many sessions your health insurance will cover. If you dream about making love to your therapist—you may wish that she would reduce her sliding scale fees.

Tongues/mouths

Dreams of tongues or mouths express your fear of participating in rap groups.

Water

Dreaming of water means you're thirsty. Get out of bed and drink a glass of water.

Zoo

Dreams of a zoo or of being surrounded by all types of animals symbolizes that your friends are thinking about you.

Rules:

O.K. campers! You remember how to play this one from when you were a kid. This game is best played in a group, the larger and rowdier the better. One person asks the other group members for the parts of speech indicated and writes them in the spaces provided. Then the completed story is read aloud to the group, resulting in, or at least contributing to, general hilarity (this is where the rowdiness is helpful). Note: There are no "right" answers!

Vacation

_____ and _____ spent their vacation together in
woman's name   **woman's name**

_____. They made sure they saw all the _____ sights:
the name of city   **adjective**

_____, the_____, and the _____ _____.
plural noun   **plural noun**   **adjective**   **noun**

They left enough time to _____, as well.   Although they did
                                        verb

_____ a few times during their _____ trip, they felt
        verb   **adjective**

_____ by the end.   After their return, all their friends said they
   adjective

looked _____ and_____.
                adjective   **adjective**

You think it's love when...
              ...you look at rings together.

You know it's love when...
              ...you buy rings for each other.

You know it's over when...
              ...you take your ring off to wash the
                        dishes and it sits by the sink for months.

Mad Women's Libs

Argument

_____ and _____ had been together _____ months,
woman's name   woman's name   number

around the time that _____-_____ set in. They found themselves
                                noun

_____ arguing about everything, from the _____ to how to
adverb   plural noun

_____ a _____. If one said _____, the other
verb   noun   color

said _____. They called each other names like _____ and
     color   noun

_____ and even sometimes _____ each other. Finally
noun   past tense verb

this _____ phase of their relationship ended and they _____
       adjective   past tense verb

_____ ever after.
    adverb

You think it's love when...
   ...you wash a couple of pairs of her underwear with your laundry.

You know it's love when...
       ...you do her laundry for her.

You know it's over when...
         ...you   shrink   her   sweater   on   purpose.

Flea Market

_____ and _____ wanted to get _____ for their
woman's name   woman's name   plural noun

_____ apartment so they went shopping at the _____ flea
adjective   adjective

market. They found everything they needed: _____ _____
                                                    adjective   plural noun

for their _____, a(n) _____ to put in their _____,
          plural noun   noun   noun

and even a(n) _____ to decorate their _____ _____.
                  noun   adjective   noun

They bought some _____ to eat and went _____ home with
                     plural noun   adverb

their purchases.

You think it's love when...
                ...her mannerisms are quaint.

You know it's love when...
                ...her mannerisms are adorable.

You know it's over when...
                ...her mannerisms drive you crazy.

Softball Game

It was the last game of the season and _____ was up to bat.

woman's name

She _____ the ball so hard that it hit the shortstop's _____.

past tense verb _____ body part

The infield _____, amazed that the _____ could travel that

past tense verb _____ noun

fast. The _____ shortstop recovered in time to pick up the

adjective

_____ and throw it to first. The umpire called the runner

noun

_____ and the crowd _____. The opposing team

adjective _____ past tense verb

_____ in disbelief, and shouted that the umpire was a(n)

past tense verb

_____ _____.

adjective _____ noun

You think it's love when...

...you're willing to hang out with her friends.

You know it's love when...

...you prefer her friends to your own.

You know it's over when...

...you like her friends better than her.

Anniversary

It was _____ and _____'s anniversary. They had been
      woman's name   woman's name

together for _____ years. Finding the _____ gift for each
        number   adjective

other was important. In past years, they had given each other _____
                                                 plural noun

and _____, but this year was to be _____. Each felt very
    plural noun   adjective

_____ about the other and so wanted to _____ the other.
  adjective   verb

After much deliberation and shopping around, they _____ ended up
                                         adverb

giving each other the _____ thing: matching _____.
                adjective   plural noun

You think it's love when...
        ...you let her pick the movie regardless of
        her taste.
You know it's love when...
        ...you think she has great taste.

You know it's over when...
        ...you watch all the movies she wouldn't let
        you watch before.

Mail-Order Fun

In the Good Vibrations catalogue, you'll find many ideas for a(n) _____

_____ fun time. There are _____ sex toys to suit everyone's
   adjective   adjective

needs. There are _____ that vibrate, using batteries or_____.
                     plural noun   plural noun

There are _____ _____ that you can strap onto your
               adjective   plural noun

_____ to enhance your lover's _____. You can
     body part   noun

even get a _____ that is so small it fits in your _____.
           noun   noun

Some _____ are made for _____ people to use together.
      plural noun   number

So fill out your order form right now for a(n) _____ time.
                                       adjective

You think it's love when...
   ...you are supportive of her softball playing.

You know it's love when...
   ...you go to all her games.

You know it's over when...
   ...you don't notice that softball season has started.

Common Lesbian Fight Lines

Are you always arguing about the same old things? If you're getting bored and redundant, use any of these tried and tested lines to begin your next fight.

"What do you mean your ex-lover's going to be there?"

"No, no, that's not how it happened."

"When we split up, I get to keep this."

"I'm confused."

"Why didn't you call?"

"You spent fifty dollars on *what*?"

"I love you more than you love me."

"I don't want to talk about it any more."

"You got to choose last time we did it."

"I'm not laughing *at* you."

"We need to talk."

"Haven't you had enough to drink?"

"Did you have to eat all those tacos?"

"Aren't those my socks you're wearing?"

"I'm not telling you how to run your life but…"

"What do you mean you want more experience?"

"What do you mean you find her attractive?

"Guess who's coming to stay next week?"

"You're more awake than I am tonight, aren't you?"

"You're going to hang *that* in the living room?"

"Well, *you* have a selective memory *don't* you?"

"Of course I don't mind if you ask her to dance."

"Now isn't a good time to discuss this."

"I don't believe you did that in front of_____."

"Thank you for letting me contribute to this decision."

"You're playing softball again tonight?"

"Let's face it, I'm right."

"Try to see it my way; only time will tell if I am right or I am wrong."

Common Lesbian Excuse Lines

"But I've always been this way."

"My therapist said I should say how I feel."

"But you know they're uncomfortable when we're affectionate in front of them."

"I just have to learn to handle stress better."

"I have my period (or cramps , PMS, water retention, etc.)."

"It's just that my tastes are different from yours."

"I never knew I was capable of this much jealousy."

"Things would be easier if you were in therapy."

"I'm just not as open as you are."

"It's nothing personal, I'm just not feeling sexual right now."

"I haven't been attracted to *anyone* lately."

"We hardly see each other ."

"It's just that I know how to handle these things better than you do."

"I'm still working through issues with my mother (or father, sibling, ex, etc)."

"I'm under a lot of pressure."

"You pushed a button."

"I'm older than you are."

"That's your problem."

"It's just that I love you so much."

"It's too hot."

"I'm tired."

"I'm confused."

"Not better, just different."

"It was my idea first."

"It just happened."

"I haven't been feeling well lately."

"I have gas."

"While you see it your way, there's a chance that we may fall apart before too long."

Common Lesbian Make Up Lines

When all else fails try one of these.

"Despite our differences, you're the best thing that's ever happened to me."

"I let my imagination run away with me."

"Lets discuss this in the bedroom."

"Aren't we blowing this out of proportion?"

"I'll try to be more patient, understanding, etc."

"We don't have to agree on everything."

"I'll watch what I eat from now on."

"You look really cute when you're angry."

"I even heated chocolate sauce for your ice cream."

"I'm not going to softball practice tonight."

"Why don't *you* choose."

"We can work it out (life is very short...)"

"How about that massage I promised you?"

"I think we handled this better than we have in the past."

"Let's stay home tonight and not tell anybody."

"We promised we'd never go to bed mad. So either we stay up or make up."

"I'm committed to making this work."

"OK, I'm listening."

"I'll feel closer to you now."

"I promise it won't happen again."

"I'm sorry."

"We really needed this talk."

"Let's give it time."

"I overreacted."

"I can see your point of view."

"I love you."

"I'm confused."

"You're supposed to laugh now."

WHEN SHE LOOKS AT YOUR FACE, WHAT DO YOU WANT HER TO SEE?

The ruddy complexion of an outdoorsy timberdyke?

The pale, fatigued face of a hard-working political activist?

The innocent, unblemished look of a newborn babydyke?

The mature, experienced look of an older, wiser lesbian?

You can choose your look from the new LESBELLINE line of facial cosmetic shading, **DYKETONES.**
Choose from these popular tones:

MOTHER EARTHY, Rosy Dykeling,
SAVE-THE-WHALES AZURE
CANVASSING KHAKI, *Wild Party Red,* Up-All-Night Red
Ms. Lesbian (for mature women)

LESBELLINE

Cosmetics for the politically-correct dyke that allow her to see only what you want her to see!

PUZZLES WITH A MESSAGE #1

To complete this acrostic, find the answers to the clues on the right—one letter per space. Solution page 109

Things to do with Nancy Drew	Clues
Why Ned wondered what to do with Nancy.	

Things to do with Nancy Drew
Why Ned wondered what to do with Nancy.

1. _ _ _S_ _ _
2. _ _ _ _ _H_ _ _ _ _ _
3. _ _ _E_ _ _ _ _ _
4. _L_ _ _
5. _O_ _
6. _ _ _V_ _ _
7. _ _ _ _E_ _ _ _ _
8. _ _ _D_ _ _ _ _
9. _ _ _ _ _ _ _G_ _ _ _
10. _ _ _ _ _E_
11. _ _O_ _ _
12. _R_ _ _ _ _
13. _ _ _G_ _ _ _ _ _ _
14. _E_ _ _ _ _ _ _

Clues

1. Dad Drew's first name
2. Where Nancy lives
3. What Nancy is
4. Nancy's favorite color
5. George's hairstyle
6. Bess's last name
7. Ned's last name
8. Nancy's style of car
9. She manages the Drew household
10. Dad Drew's occupation
11. Nancy's hair color
12. Those who Nancy often catches
13. How Bess usually feels when she helps Nancy
14. The name of it is at the end of every book

You think it's love when...
...you lend her a ten.

You know it's love when...
...you co-sign a loan for her.

You know it's over when...
...you take her to small claims court.

PUZZLES WITH A MESSAGE #2

Types of Inner space Solution page 109

What the process of going inward is	Clues
1._ _ _ _ _ _ _ _ _ G_ _ _ _ _	1. In with others (2 words)
2. _ _ _ _ _ _ _ _ E _ _ _ _ _ _	2. In-tuitive/Interpretation (2 words)
3. _ _ _ _ _ _ _ _ T _ _ _ _	3. Alone in a dark place (2 words)
4. _ _ _ _ _ T_ _ _ _ _ _	4. In the smell (2 words)
5. _ _ _ _ I _ _ _ _ _ _ _ _ _	5. In the muscles (2 words)
6. _ _ _ N_ _ _ _	6. In the unconscious
7. _ _ G_ _ _ _ _ _	7. In the past
8. _ _ _ _ _ T_ _ _ _ _ _	8. In the water
9. _ _ _ _ _ O_ _ _ _ _ _	9. In the mind
10. _ _ _ K _ _ _ _ _	10. Call in (2 words)
11. _ _ N	11. In the East
12. _ _ _ _ O_ _ _ _	12. In the stars
13 _ _ _ _ _ _ _ W_	13. Tune in (2 words)
14. _ _ M_ _ _ _ _ _ _	14. In the numbers
15. _ _ _ _ _ _ E_ _ _ _ _ _ _	15. In print (3words)

You think it's love when...
...you think about her when she's away.

You know it's love when...
...you read the daily weather reports for where she is.
You know it's over when...
...you hope it rains where she is.

PUZZLES WITH A MESSAGE #3

TELEVISION MOTHERS   Solution page 109

Television Mothers Of The Past	Clues
Two required characteristics	*What actresses played these TV moms*
1. — — —P — — — — — — —	1. Ruth McDevitt's role
2. — — — — — — — — — —R —	2. Alice Mitchell
3. — — — — — —E — —	3. Donna Stone
4. — — — —T — — — — — — — —	4. Laura Petrie
5. — — — — — — —T —	5. Margaret Anderson
6. — — — — — — —Y — — — — —	6. Peggy Riley
7. — — — — — A — — — — — — — — — —	7. June Cleaver
8. — — —N — — — — —	8. Margaret Williams
9. — — — — —D — —	9. Doris Martin
10. — —P — — — — — —	10. Carolyn Muir
11 — — — — — — — —E — — — — — — —	11. Carol Brady
12. — — — — — — —R — — —	12. Marion Cunningham
13. — — — — — —F — — — —	13. Mrs. Remington
14. —E— — — — — —	14. Natalie Lane
15. — — — — — C— — — —	15. Elinore Hathaway
16. — — — — — — —T — — — — — —	16. Ozzie's wife

23

PUZZLES WITH A MESSAGE #4

Leading Ladies Of The Past   Solution page 109

How they acted	Clues
1. G _ _ _ _	1.In the1933 movie *Queen Christina*
2. _ R _ _ _ _	2. Lesbian movie director
3. _ E _ _	3. Wasn't afraid to defend gays - *She Done Him Wrong*
4. _ A _ _ _	4. First lady of the theater
5. _ _ _ T _ _ _ _ _	5. Kissed a woman *Morocco* in -1930
6. _ _ _ _ _ _ _ R _ _ _ _	6.Tough lesbian in *Touch of Evil* - l958
7. _ _ _ _ _ O _ _	7. Rancher in *Johnny Guitar* - 1954
8. _ _ _ _ _ _ L _ _	8. Was believed a lesbian (first name)
9. _ E _ _ _ _ _	9. Always wore slacks to work
10. _ _ _ _ M _ _	10. Star of *Casa Blanca*
11. _ _ _ _ _ O _ _	11. Started United Artist - 1919
12. D _ _ _ _	12.. Known for playing strong women
13. _ _ _ E _	13. Our Miss Brooks
14. _ _ _ L _ _ _	14. Wrote script of *The Children's Hour*
15. _ _ S _	15. Directed cast and acted in 1920 *Scarlet letter*

You think it's love when...
        ...you try the food she likes.

You know it's love when...
        ...you love the food she likes.

You know it's over when...
        ...the sight of that food makes you sick.

More Television Mothers   Solution page 109

Characteristics of 'new and improved' mothers	Which Actresses played these characters?
1. _ _ _ _ _ Ⓞ _ _ _ _ _ _	1. the mother's voice, My Mother the Car
2. _ _ _ _ _ _ _ Ⅾ _ _ _ _ _ _ _	2. Lily Munster
3. _ _ _ _ Ⅾ _ _ _ _ _ _ _	3. Alice Hyatt
4. _ _ _ _ _ _ _ _ Ⓐ _ _ _ _ _ _ _	4. Edith Bunker
5. _ _ Ⓝ _ _ _ _ _ _ _	5. Ida Morgenstern
6. _ _ _ _ _ _ _ _ _ _ Ⅾ _ _ _ _	6. Alice Kramden
7. _ _ _ _ _ _ _ _ _ _ _ Ⅾ _ _ _ _	7. Louise Jefferson
8. _ _ _ _ _ _ _ _ Ⓤ _	8. Maude
9. _ _ _ _ _ _ _ Ⓝ _ _ _ _ _ _	9. Morticia Addams
10 _ _ _ _ _ _ _ _ _ Ⓝ _ _ _ _ _	10. Ann Romano("Ms.")
11. _ _ Ⓨ _ _ _ _ _ _ _ _	11. Kaye Buel

You think it's love when...

...you know her zip code.

You know it's love when...

...you know her Social Security number.

You know it's over when...

...you have to look up her phone number.

PUZZLES WITH A MESSAGE #6

Challenger—Our Bookstores Solution page 109

1. _ _ _ _ _ _ _ _ _ _ S _ _ _ _ _ _ _ _ _ _ _
2. _ _ _ _ _ _ _ T _ _ _ _
3. _ _ _ _ _ _ _ E _
4. _ _ _ _ _ _ _ _ _ A _ _ _ _ _ _ _ _
5. _ _ M _ _ _ _ _ _ _
6. _ _ _ _ _ Y _ _ _ _ _ _ _ _ _ _ _ _ _ _
7. _ _ _ _ _ S _ _ _ _ _ _ _ _ _
8. _ _ _ _ _ E _ _ _ _
9. _ _ _ _ _ _ _ _ X _ _ _ _ _
10. _ _ _ _ S _ _ _ _ _
11. _ _ _ _ _ C _ _ _ _ _
12. _ _ _ E _ _ _ _ _ _ _ _ _ _ _
13. _ _ _ _ _ N _ _ _ _ _ _ _ _
14. _ _ _ _ _ _ E _ _ _ _ _ _ _ _ _ _ _ _ _
15. _ _ _ _ _ _ S _ _ _ _
16. _ _ _ A _ _ _ _ _ _ _ _ _ _ _ _ _ _
17. _ _ _ _ _ _ _ R
18. _ _ _ _ _ _ E _ _ _ _ _ _ _ _ _ _
19. _ _ _ _ _ _ _ B _ _ _ _
20. _ _ _ _ _ _ _ _ _ _ _ E _ _ _ _ _
21. _ _ _ _ _ _ _ S _ _ _ _ _ _ _ _ _ _ _ _ _ _ _
22. _ _ _ _ _ _ T _ _ _ _ _ _ _ _ _ _ _ _
23. _ _ _ _ _ _ _ R _ _ _ _ _ _ _ _ _ _
24. _ _ _ _ _ E _ _ _ _ _ _
25. _ _ _ _ _ _ A _ _ _ _
26. _ _ _ _ D _ _ _ _ _ _ _ _
27. _ _ _ _ _ I _ _ _ _ _ _ _ _
28. _ _ _ _ _ N _ _ _ _ _ _ _ _ _ _ _ _ _ _
29. _ _ _ _ _ _ _ B _ _ _ _ _ _ _
30. _ _ _ _ E _ _ _ _ _ _ _ _ _
31. _ _ _ _ _ _ _ D _ _ _ _ _

PUZZLES WITH A MESSAGE #6

Here are the addresses of bookstores in the U.S. and Canada, you supply the names.
(From *Places of Interest to Women*, Ferrari Publications, PO box 37887 Phoenix AZ, 85069)

1. 250 Cowan Road, Gulfport MS
2. 1009 Valencia St., San Francisco CA
3. 2625 E. 12th Ave., Denver Co
4. 600 Frenchmen St., New Orleans LA
5. 1617 N. 32nd St. #5, Phoenix AZ
6. 425 E. 31st St., Baltimore MD
7. 1426 21st St. NW, Washington DC
8. 512 S. Main St., Moscow ID
9. 1029 E. 11th Ave., Denver CO
10. 2020-B 11th Ave. S., Birmingham AL
11. 1295 Bardstown Rd., Louisville KY
12. 1967 N. Halsted St., Chicago IL
13. 1612 Harmon Pl., Minneapolis MN
14. 168 Elmwood Ave., Buffalo NY
15. 680 Washington St., New York NY
16. 61 Haywood St., Asheville NC
17. 357 Commercial St., Provincetown MA
18. 1501 Belmont Ave., Seattle WA
19. 438 Main St., Rockland ME
20. 68 W. Palisade Ave., Englewood NJ
21. 1003 E. Carson, Pittsburgh PA
22. 915 State St., New Haven CT
23. 6536 Telegraph Ave., Oakland CA
24. 65 S. 4th St., Columbus OH
25. 828 E. 64th St., Indianapolis IN
26. 7545 Biscayne Blvd., Miami FL
27. 2205 Silver Ave. SE, Albuquerque NM
28. 1065 N. 33rd St., Lincoln NE
29. 186 Hampshire St., Cambridge MA
30. 1070 Lawrence St., Eugene OR
31. 5 Kivy St., Huntington Station NY

Lesbian Authors   Solution page 109

What these authors have	Books
1. _ _ C _ _ _ _ _ _	1. Mrs. Porter's Letter
2. _ _ _ H _ _ _	2. Stoner McTavish
3. _ A _ _	3. Bittersweet
4. _ _ R _ _ _ _ _ _	4. The Cruise
5. _ A _ _ _ _	5. The Color Purple
6. _ C _ _ _ _ _ _	6. After Dolores
7. _ _ _ _ _ _ T	7. Beverly Malibu
8. _ _ _ E	8. Memory Board
9. _ _ _ R _ _ _ _	9. The Latecomer
10. _ _ _ _ S _ _	10. Trash

You think it's love when...

...you read her horoscope.

You know it's love when...

...you read her horoscope first.

You know it's over when...

...you forget what sign she is.

A closet that is a temporary stage for some and a way of life for others. This lesbian will go out of her way to appear straight to anyone and everyone. (Ever see Kristy McNichol on the Arsenio Hall Show?) She is likely to cover her walls with posters of the latest male hunk or Anita Bryant-look alikes. She votes Republican. Often her conversations include vague references to 'friends', and she may even switch pronouns on Monday morning when talking about her weekend. She believes that no one could possibly suspect that she is gay. In actuality, everyone knows.

She has a strong network of lesbian and gay friends, but all of her social life is limited to the gay community. She goes to women's concerts only, gay bars only, lesbian social groups only, and all of her friends are gay or lesbian. She would never consciously consider herself a separatist, but when pressed, can't name one friend who is not gay. The little interaction she has with the straight world, such as work and family, is tolerated but not fully participated in. Most likely, outside the community no one knows she is gay; they just think she is a loner.

THE OPEN CLOSET

A closet is just a closet—a place to leave all the politically correct black shoes, purple ties and natural cottons. It is not some place to hide, nor a platform to proclaim from. Just a closet, like anybody's closet. This style of "out" is when being gay is part of self identity, not all of it. "Yeah, I'm a lesbian, just another lesbian."

FLASHING NEON CLOSET

This is one screaming lesbian. In her lifestyle, every moment is an opportunity to come out to somebody. She will go out of her way to draw attention to the fact that she is a lesbian, either visually or verbally. Her closet is an opportunity for advertisement of the fact that she is gay and she uses it like a billboard. One can often hear her saying any time or place, "As a lesbian, I take offense to that!"

WHAT CLOSET?

In this scenario, lesbian lifestyle seems to be a matter of semantics. Is there a closet to hide in if that concept is unspoken? (Maybe it's an existential matter!) What do you call women who have lived their lives together, sharing their hearts, their home and their lives' work, but who don't consider themselves "lesbians"? This type of woman may be heard exclaiming, "I am not a lesbian! I'm just in love with Janice!"

COMING OUT

**You may know you're a lesbian.
And you may think that's all you need to know.
BUT YOU'RE WRONG,
TODAY THAT JUST ISN'T ENOUGH!**

EVERYONE wants to know you're a lesbian–your family, your employer, your landlord, your friends, your coworkers, your cat, your governor, your trash collector, your creditors, the kid at the cash register at the 7-11, Ophrah Winfrey, and many more who interact with you on a daily basis.

The **WANNA BE GAY** Psychologist's Collective knows how important it is for you to be open about your lifestyle. So we've designed **COMING OUT** Kits that help you share your sexual preference with others.

☆ **COMING OUT** AT HOME
 helps your family members know about your lesbianism through a video tape that shows them what a lesbian looks like.

☆ **COMING OUT** AT WORK
 is a motivational presentation for employers and coworkers, with flow charts and account sheets, that details vital statistics about lesbians on the work force and their behaviors in the ladies' washroom.

☆ **COMING OUT** TO SALES CLERKS AND OTHERS
 offers advice in dealing with those who you want to give your money to, but who treat you like shit when you do.

☆ **COMING OUT** ON NATIONAL TELEVISION
 is a self–help booklet and video tape that helps you choose the right colors for your on–the–air revelations and the proper tone of voice for making your pronouncement.

THE
COMING OUTKITS
when you think **they** need to know.

"Quotables"

Simply unscramble each of the words horizontally to unearth a famous or infamous female quote. Here is an example. Solutions page 110

Queen Victoria said,

"EW RAE ONT DMAUES"   *ANSWER—We are not amused.*

 # 1 Bette Midler said,

"I MA HITERNEVYG   UOY EEWR DARAFI RUYO TTELLI
GLRI DOWLU ORGW PU OT EB —NAD RYUO TITLEL YOB."

 # 2 Elayne Boosler said,

"DUL'TWON TI EB AREGT FI OUY DOCUL YOLN TGE DSIA
RMOF IIGVGN OEYNM OT IISVENETLO HERACRPSE?"

 # 3 Muriel Spark in *The Prime of Miss Jean Brodie* said,

"VIGE EM A GRLI AT NA SSRAEIOELPIBMN GEA ADN HES
SI EINM RFO FELI."

 # 4 Robin Tyler, referring to Anita Bryant said,

"TNIAA , UYO EAR OT YTTIIAHSNCIR   HWAT TINAP — YB—
RMSNUBE SI OT RAT."

 # 5 Dolly Parton said,

"TSI' A OODG GNHTI AHTT I SAW RONB A NWMOA. OR D'I
VEAH ENEB A GRAD EUENQ."

36

REMEMBER WHAT HAPPENED TO YOU LAST SUMMER?

You met that attractive woman at your friend's barbecue while your burger was on the grill. The time was right, the temperature was perfect – but how were you to know that the woman was a strict vegetarian who wouldn't be caught dead with a meat–eater like you??

So when you bit into your bloody–rare burger
right in front of her horrified face,
it was good riddance to you!

Don't let this happen again! This summer take along
FAKESTEAK™.

ACT UP

ANNIE OAKLEY

RADCLYFFE HALL

TOFU PUPS
PERRIER
RICE DREAM

SAPPHO

39

Word Search 1

Let's start off easy. Here is the basic straight forward word search, complete with word listing. Words can be in any direction, horizontal, vertical, diagonal, and in reverse order. This one is on a subject we can all relate to no matter how we define them. Solution on page 110

Families

Singleparent
Interreligious
Twoincome
Blended
Communal
Dualcareer
Egalitarian
Extended
Foster
Interethnic
Interracial
Nuclear
Surrogate

```
U N E P E M G S B T S T D B C Y X O U U
L U S K M B W D U D P U Q U R T Q N G F
A C E U W E X R P R A H T P G P C N F U
I L F O O H Y X I L R L Y E I D C Y X Y
C E X O G I L Q C C W O A L U X Q Y B T
A A O N S F G A N L I A G U A C L B Z W
R R T I X T R I B H T N G A O Y A P K O
R P U D T E E E L K M W H M T X M Y N I
E M I I E N K R C E Z T M T B E U A G N
T X K R X M E G H M R U U K E X I W N C
N U A K M Q U R B R N R M B G R X M U O
I C O E D M O L A A H H E U A X E D U M
K Q N K T U E C L P P Q P T I K E T A E
O T H E E N U X E T E U I M N K T B N X
M C X H D U B S J J Z L F E U I M Y H I
T L O E M U Q M A B A U G C X B U U B Z
Y Y D T O X J K U G A R Z N J P Y J L F
I P P B W J C O E X Q W U B I Y X S T X
W F R B Y O X F D G M U W A L S J O W S
T E L A E R K I E X T E N D E D L B B M
```

Word Search 2

We're still starting off easy, but now the word list contains titles of novels by Ruth Rendell. The good news is the word list is still provided; the bad news is each title you need to search for can be anywhere from 1 to 4 words long. Words are only listed horizontally, vertically, or diagonally. Solution on page 110

From Doom With Death
Heartstones
Judgment in Stone
Killing Doll
Death Notes
Fever Tree
Live Flesh
Lake Of Darkness

Master of the Moor
Shake Hands Forever
Sleeping Life
Speaker of Mandarin
Tree of Hands
Unkindness Of Ravens
Vanity Dies Hard
Wolf to the Slaughter

Ruth Rendell

```
W U S H A K E H A N D S F O R E V E R G
O N F L M A S T E R O F T H E M O O R G
L K R D A V R H T K N H U I R Y S F W S
F I H P U K F C L P L A B X Z Z U Z R P
T N S X T R E E O F H A N D S D H R V E
O D L Q N B V O O D D G R T N E O W X A
T N E E V I E L F W D P T U T A V Z K K
H E E V R Z R G Y D V J E R S T F C E E
E S P P R X T L X E A H K E W H V J C R
S S I V I U R C Q Z S R N G E N Q P M O
L O N F Y L E Y V E T O K O M O C G Z F
A F G R Q P E A L Z T K B N Y T B M M M
U R L W F G G F X S K J O J E E Q C E A
G A I G J F E Y T B I L Q B D S T H P N
H V F G G V G R V G L T D R O X S Z I D
T E E T I C A Z K I L L I N G D O L L A
E N G L L E R O F Y L J A R O F H P R R
R S P B H V A N I T Y D I E S H A R D I
J U D G M E N T I N S T O N E P C E Y N
X F R O M D O O M W I T H D E A T H W I
```

41

Now it's time to get serious. This word search contains twelve titles of novels written by Margaret Atwood. This time no word list is provided. How many titles can you remember or find within the puzzle? Words are only listed horizontally, vertically, or diagonally. Solutions and word list on page 111

Margaret Atwood

```
Q J E T I Z I S G W L E I I U K U U N J K
W T C A I A D F D L H S E S E U E B P X E
Y G W W Z X A H Q D C S R L P I D D F S B
M F N O A D B N X R P U A I M P I D X G O
D Y R K H O D M U A S T K R U Z B U L U B
B F R S G E H O T O S U A B M F L C N E X
Z N U C A A G F D S H R S O T E C W W P
P U O G U A N D I D Y B L R S R W U I Y M
R S S B W P T A E L T R N C O U O C J L G
J U N K F B M S I D I D I G N E M S Y S J
R R J N I D C D E G P T W U K S A C X O C
G F E D N W O H G Y I O Z B L T N A Z U I
R A J A I B L N N L E R E W L O A M N Q R
J C H U U Q I U O G Y M Q M Q R J C Q Y C
D I Z G C C O P W E W W K U S I F H R H L
C N R P N J R E W C E G Q X U E E F M X E
Z G X A G E Z L G X J H J I W S D J P A G
B J D K W X J D S F Q N B Y L J G A D H A
U Q C O I I G L N Y U A K G J T U J B E M
U Q P L I F E B E F O R E M A N L G J B E
G C W K Q A S E L A D Y O R A C L E Q W J
```

Clueless Word Search 4

Welcome to the 90s'! This puzzle contains 30 terms associated with the computer. Again, no word list is provided. Words are listed in any direction, horizontally, vertically, diagonally, and in reverse order. Solutions and word list on page 111

Computers

```
T F N B W J S T G N I Z I L A I T I N I F A
E H S A R C H D E M X N G P Q T G A E J A J
W U G J D K A R X C T D P A I B Z S C M R T
H D Y F S H A P U E U E T S O H Y N L E M F
A L G P Z W Y A G F C B M S Z U R B T X E D
R Q W Z T E B R H U Y U J W P F W U A T Z X
D D K F F J A A R T D G T O G O P R E U U G
W B O I S T Y S E I K G R R X M S L D U D T
A S R D E T O N S O Z I P D O B E G O E J R
R K S D A R S K J T T N R C I D B N C C G O
E E I A F F C M T A O G O L H G X I U A N B
B B S S M G H L R P H R R U Q H Q M M F I A
X O D A I X A R E N C K R H W S U M E R T U
E G O I B N B R I I L W E D L B J A N E I U
S L Y T I A A C M S E I P P O L F R T T D H
H R O M I T T D E G U J G B D U G G A N E M
N U R O I N B A Q M F E F F P E Z O T I O E
A E H N P U G J D S T H Y C U B M R I F N M
T U G K S W S O L Y A O P A A S U P O Q U O
U J L A I T N E U Q E S S U Y C Z L N O S R
O C O M P A T I B I L E W Z K G M F P J Z Y
T Y P E S E T T I N G W A G T I U C R I C U
```

Clueless Word Search 5

For those of you who need a second chance, there are 14 titles of novels written by Marge Piercy hidden in this puzzle. Titles can be up to 6 words long. Remember- the puzzle does not contain punctuation (even if the title does). Words are only listed vertically, horizontally, and diagonally. Solutions and word list on page 111

Marge Piercy

```
F W H R D T F O F J N Q M T P C H S D J E L
H O I X C A B I Z J J M O G G H I T P J L I
K M G U Q U N R Q Q H P L L U P B K R K F U
F A H F L Y A W A Y H O M E X B X E C Q B I
A N C O A K E F H I W H D N C H T N S B D N
K O O G R P L X O M D S U E Z A B J W S Q G
E N S T J M T R J M Q E L U W G Y A C T M I
P T T U T M Y F L P X P D E F M R A Z O F N
Y H O B W H J M X F O B H L A C I P T N I T
H E F K R D J M O E W T M C I U N S B E G H
A E L Q T E J G P T N J D C Y U A N F P G E
R D I E F M A R A O H M U K H F E N Q A D O
D G U K W S E K S Z M E L B N D D S M P W P
L E I F S M A E I I O R R W R Q L B L E J E
O O N B M Z L G O N E T O S O L D I E R S N
U F G U M C U N J N G D A T B H A B S K U Q
I T S C R Q G U X J G C N C X O K I H N N E
N I E I P X I Q B N F F A X N X D J N I U U
G M C A P W E Z I A H X L M R U W Y B F R S
R E R W M F S O G E T F Q D P J R A G E F Q
J G Q A R R G J Y A J W K O Y D W C B Z F S
L J S M A L L C H A N G E S I R Q L N M F F
```

44

Time now to separate the women from the girls. In this puzzle you are provided with a list of twelve titles of books popular with lesbian readers. You must provide the name of the authors to create the word list for this puzzle. The first one has been completed for you. Solutions and word list on page 112

Book	Author
The Color Purple	Alice Walker
The Children of the Albatross	.............................?
Celestial Navigation	
Jane and Prudence	
As the Road Curves	
Optimist's Daughter	
Women of Brewster Place	
Vida	
The Heart of a Woman	
Sudden Death	
Song of Solomon	
To the Lighthouse	

Matching-fiction

```
N I U T O N I M O R R I S O N W D S
G E O K T T N A E U Z R U S R O X E
M R H U B C S C H T O U U E K U Y U
Y E P M X T N S M L N T K L F Y I D
F J L H U S P M Y T K L A L G M O O
M W U I T A T A Z Z A Z O Q Z A W R
Q I C N Z T N U T W U W R U N R C A
B E I F T A R E E O A E R R U G W W
A A J N I N B C L I L Q Y U P E B E
O W R R T A I E N Y O Y R X Q P F L
N O O B Z L G I T A N A I S N I N T
W L P S A N G E U H I L K L U E X Y
G C A U A R N J S K D E U T R R R U
I O S A I N A Q D M D E H Q K C U A
I S Y U A T P P S W E U A C G Y S E
Q A Z T U T C Q Y R Q M C N I G·R X
M E Y E T B T H W M X I K S Q O R K
R I T A M A E B R O W N D H G P W J
```

45

Never again will you be able to look at 'straight' puzzle books in the same way. This puzzle features twenty actresses popular on TV. You are provided with the character's name and the show; you must provide the name of the actress to complete the word search list. This first one has been completed for you. Solution on page 112

Character	Show	Actress
Jessica Fletcher	Murder She Wrote	Angela Lansbury
June Cleaver	Leave it to Beaver	.................................?
Jeannie	I Dream of Jeannie	
Della Street	Perry Mason	
"Ma" Barkley	The Big Valley	
Maude Findley	Maude	
Colleen McMurphy	China Beach	
Julia Baker	Julia	
Julia Sugarbaker	Designing Women	
Samantha Stevens	Bewitched	
Marilyn McGrath	Heartbeat	
Margaret Houlihan	M.A.S.H.	
Lucy Ricardo	Lucy Ball	
Anne Marie	That Girl	
Julie Barnes	MOD Squad	
Sally Rogers	The Dick Van 'Dyke' Show	
Sister Bertrille	The Flying Nun	
Grace Van Owen	L.A. Law	
Emily Hartley	The Bob Newhart Show	
Rhoda Morgenstern	The Mary Tyler Moore Show	

TV Ladies

```
L I B T N D P R N C Y U U W X U K P C B F W Z
U D B K K X I C O I D C F E X K D Y L A B G G
C O E J A P G A R S Y N K X C H Y G O R A E Z
Y C K W U Z K U H U E R Q Y C R Y R R B R L G
B D F Y W A H K I A C M W U U B U M E A B I A
A S H H E T L U B U N N A B L U X Z T R A Z I
L A O L R F N E I D A N S R D N O J T A R A L
L D N A I J O S R T H N C A I I X R A B A B S
U H A P B O G X S I A I Q A B E Q N S I E E T
W E Y A K F W A Z L E M T C R Z P H W L D T R
B M P A B A R B A R A H A L E R A K I L E H I
P Y A T B A M L I K Y D A L W P O I T I N M C
E N B R B J E D X P Y U I R H J K L T N I O K
G W Q R L G E N I N Z I E X P X E K L G Q N L
G Z A U N O N C A P I A K P I E E U C S O T A
Y B K A C U T L F E R E J O T E R U Z L E G N
L D T W Y C E H S U S A N D E Y C Q I Y Y O D
I L J G R D U Q O J A M N R L S N A X M E M M
P I H F A W R L P M W H C Q A L H K R H Z E L
T F P N C B S K U A A K J S O H S K N T S R K
O X A O W I P U N W Y S H X P R S E R R E Y S
N D L A A T W S A L L Y F I E L D U S X N R U
S U Z A N N E P L E S H E T T E O U O F Q Z B
```

Take A Hint — Word Search 8

Is she or isn't she? This puzzle contains the names of twenty actresses who have portrayed lesbians or bisexuals in movies. You are provided with the name of the movie and the number of actresses names you are looking for. The first one has been completed for you. Solutions and word list on page 112

Movie	Actress	Movie	Actress
The Rose	Bette Midler	The Children's Hour (2)	?
A Question of Love		Waiting for the Moon	
A Young Man and a Horn		The Killing of Sister George (2)	
Desert Hearts (2)		Manhattan	
Silkwood		Persona	
Personal Best (2)		My Two Loves (2)	
The Color Purple (2)		Handmaid's Tale	

Only Acting

```
P S O U Z R U U C D M L Y N N R E D G R A U E X D
A M A R R I E T T E H A R T L E Y M B T S Y L D P
T M Q W L E M B D X R M A R G A R E T A U E R Y A
R U A B H Q Q K P E D S E E W Y P U W R A O Z Y T
I D C R O U B D L R N Q R D I I D Z R P T G L Z R
C W K R I P U D F S T X U X A R W I A S Y T P M I
I T B E T E I O H E U S L R W B E R Y L R E I D C
A L H F K M L G E L F S T L H R C H Y R Y L R X E
C A A G E X A H L A A B A M F E L Q S P P I U S D
H Q U T S G Q S E E F U U N R M W X C D X Z W H O
A J T D I N J U N M E K R E N F Y J Y N A A H I N
R E I U R K X Y S M I H D E F A R U A U R B O R N
B N E A H E X P H N T N Y Y N P H B S K M E O L E
O X G K M H Y G A W A J G P K B D Y P M U T P E L
N I B X N N X H U X Z A E W K Z A H O Y C H I Y L
N M Q Y S Y X F E L D E D P A F W C D R D M G M Y
E O P C H E R L R P R G P A B Y G Z A T K C O A S
A A U C M P A I J T B Z G Y U F P O N L F G L C A
U I J E M E F F S X W U J H P C J U A M L O D L H
X W E M N U B L X G X S R E Q J H Q T Q I U B A B
J U K A N U Y G O L L W U N K A F J K R D E E I C
L M J N Q R Z R M Y J I N O D N I Y J P H R R N W
J N K P E B Q R U N U U G N S Y J S T N J N G E Y
M X Q M J E L J E U J I I U H H I G G K O R I H Z
K L I U U L M A N L J L W K B G K T F O N Z D A G
```

CONNECT THE DYKES

The object of this exercise is to test your ability to identify and distinguish between different (stereo) types of lesbians. We have provided you with six pictures of various kinds of lesbians. Your mission (should you choose to accept it) is to match an item from each category with the pictures. After you have completed the exercise, you can further amuse yourself by identifying which type you or your friends resemble the most. Or you can study the various types to help you decide which clothing or hairstyles are most appropriate for going out on the town or to work. You can also use the exercise as an aid in locating certain kinds of lesbians and knowing what to say to them once you have found them. Answers page 97-108

The descriptions of categories are on pages:

1)___ Identification

2)___ Description

3)___ Accoutrements

4)___ Habitat

5)___ Transportation

6)___ Common expressions

7)___ Last book read

8)___ Heroine

9)___ Social group or professional affiliation

1)___ Identification

2)___ Description

3)___ Accoutrements

4)___ Habitat

5)___ Transportation

6)___ Common expressions

7)___ Last book read

8)___ Heroine

9)___ Social group or
professional affiliation

1)___ Identification

2)___ Description

3)___ Accoutrements

4)___ Habitat

5)___ Transportation

6)___ Common expressions

7)___ Last book read

8)___ Heroine

9)___ Social group or
professional affiliation

54

1)____ Identification

2)____ Description

3)____ Accoutrements

4)____ Habitat

5)____ Transportation

6)____ Common expressions

7)____ Last book read

8)____ Heroine

9)____ Social group or
professional affiliation

1)____ Identification

2)____ Description

3)____ Accoutrements

4)____ Habitat

5)____ Transportation

6)____ Common expressions

7)____ Last book read

8)____ Heroine

9)____ Social group or
professional affiliation

1)___ Identification

2)___ Description

3)___ Accoutrements

4)___ Habitat

5)___ Transportation

6)___ Common expressions

7)___ Last book read

8)___ Heroine

9)___ Social group or professional affiliation

1) Identification —Label that Lesbian

A) Cosmodyke, B) Campus Dyke, C) Execudyke, D) Leather Dyke E) Fused Couple, F) Lesbian Mother

2) Description

A) This woman may look a little scary. Her outfit may consist of a leather vest with nothing on underneath it and skin tight leather pants, or maybe chaps over jeans with a red handkerchief protruding from the left rear pocket. On her feet are blunt-toed or silver tipped black 'fuck you' boots. She may also adorn herself with a silver studded black leather belt and bracelet (maybe even a collar). Her hair is cropped short and she wears a Muir cap set at a rakish angle. Tiny silver handcuffs are earring possibilities and she has at least one tattoo.

56

B) There may be a wide variation in appearance, but the members of each set resemble each other. This resemblance tends to increase as the relationship develops. They have identical haircuts, identical clothes, (in fact problems may arise when they can't remember whose clothes are whose) identical jewelry (given lovingly to each other), etc. The strong resemblance between these two lesbians often causes straight people to ask, "Are you two sisters?"

C) After much research, debate, time, and money this lesbian finally became pregnant through artificial insemination. Having a child in her life is not only a personal satisfaction, but is also a political statement. She knew what would be involved to enroll her child in school and dealing with her family members and other parents at the PTA. But she may not have been prepared for the pure physical exhaustion a little dyke-tyke came with. She is often easy to recognize by her exhausted appearance and the forgotten stain of natural fruit jelly on her shirt. Her constant companion is her child, appropriately attired in politically correct T-shirts and little Birkenstock sandals.

D) This is a Lesbian version of the Charlie Girl, a sophisticated woman-about-town who knows what she wants and how to get it. Whatever is currently in vogue, she is into. She dresses in the height of fashion with such confidence and style that she can get away with wearing clothes which on another woman would actually look ugly. Only Astor Place (the birthplace of American punk haircuts) will suffice for her ultra-short haircut. This is the type of woman who literally wouldn't be caught dead in Birkenstocks. Even seeing people wearing them, especially with socks, makes her nauseous.

E) This intense young woman has a fairly distinct style. Her haircut is always on the cutting edge of fashion in some type of dramatic schizophrenic affair. Her clothing follows suit—oversized men's shirts with skin tight mini skirts. She wants to be announced before she enters a room, and she accomplishes this by her appearance. This sense of the dramatic is evident in her life. When she is involved in something, her participation is complete and passionate. She not only cares for the whales (porpoises, animals, people, etc), but she insists that every one else should care as well.

.F) This Lesbian is readily identifiable in her execudrag—a slightly feminized version of the man's business suit. Her no-nonsense haircut is short enough to be out of her way, yet long enough to keep her from appearing radical. A few things give her away as a Lesbian—give a clue about what lurks behind this male-glorified exterior—the several empty holes in her ear lobes in addition to the two filled will gold and pearl studs, and the fact that the fingernails on her first two fingers of her right hand have been carefully shortened on an otherwise manicured hand.

3) Accoutrements

A) Everything vital for life survival in the big city can be found in the large, leather shoulder bag she carries everywhere—books, cosmetics, bus tokens, underwear, clothing changes, a toothbrush—anything that she may need at any time of the day, the night, or possibly the next morning.

B) She is armed with all-purpose massive shoulder bags filled with everything she may possibly need: toys, babywipes, Heather Bishop tapes, and a softball glove sticky with apple juice.

C) She is rarely seen without her briefcase which contains the *Wall Street Journal*, *Working Woman* magazine, calculator, Cross pen set, and the ever important calendar book. For trips out of town she totes a lap top computer. At home she works on her terminal via the modem to her office and her nationwide business network.

D) Accoutrements may vary from couple to couple, but internally are the same. Identical knapsacks, identical softball gloves—even identical pets!

E) This lesbian realizes the importance of accessorizing. She usually has a variety of sex aids readily available: silk ties, nipple clamps, handcuffs, leather straps and dildos.

F) This is a person who loves to wear large jewelry. Her watch is huge—at least one wrist is covered with bangle bracelets. Her earrings seem to follow the same two-toned effect as her haircut with exceedingly large earrings in one side and small studs or crystals in the other. Over her shoulder she carries the required large leather knapsack stuffed to the gills with text books, note paper, CDs with a portable player and the latest issue of *Premier* magazine.

4) Habitat

A) This type of Lesbian can be found in meetings, in front of computer terminals, at airports and in restaurants having power lunches.

B) Found either singly or in groups, on college campuses everywhere. She may physically be in a small state college in rural Tennessee, but in her heart and attitude she is in downtown Boston or San Francisco.

C) May be found anywhere: grocery stores, concerts, campgrounds. Whenever you find one, the other isn't far away.

D) Probably seen in a natural food store laden with kids—her bag of goodies, and all her groceries and supplies piled into her net shopping bags—trying to pacify her screaming child.

E) The chic shopping centers in any city in the U.S. or abroad. She is usually seen at the theater, outdoor cafes, foreign film theaters and in line for the Mapplethorpe exhibit.

F) She can be found hanging out at any gay bar with pool tables and more than one motorcycle parked outside or at head shops that feature sex toys.

5)Transportation

A) A motorcycle, (not less than five hundred c.c.s), preferably a Harley.

B) Her ideal form of transportation is a small station wagon or a practical hatchback that will accommodate her small arsenal of daily supplies: wagons, strollers, groceries and little playmates. More times than not her car has that lived-in appearance; its floor littered with all-natural Cheerios, toys and a long-forgotten pacifier.

C) A BMW, of course.

D) If she is anywhere near a city she is completely at home using any type of public-transportation. If she can afford to own a car it is most likely a recently repainted, beat up old VW bug.

E)She knows how to get to Hawaii and back on public transportation.

F) This is the one area in which they differ. Because they are actually two people, (although discerning this may be difficult at times) their vehicles vary for practical reasons. For example, one may own a sports car (that seats two) for going out and looking cool, while the other may have a pickup truck with bucket seats for transporting a rototiller or going to the dump—and looking cool. But whichever vehicle one is driving the other usually goes along.

6) Common Expressions

A) "I have to work late." "I'm going to have to cancel." "Let's do lunch sometime." " I'll have my secretary call your secretary."

B) This is a literal term for those lesbians who are known for finishing each others sentences. They tend to speak in unison.

C) "Damn I missed my bus!" " Yo taxi."

D) When in the presence of her child this lesbian is often heard saying, "Wipe your nose" or "Do you have to go to the bathroom now?" When among adults she talks about her kid—Only her kid.

E) "But if you only understood the plight of_____ you would agree with me!"

F) "Top or bottom?"

7) Last Book Read

A) Aloud together—*Lesbian Couples* by D. Merille Lunis and G. Dorsey Green.

B) *Pure Lust* by Mary Daly

C) Whatever is number one on the New York Times best seller list

D) *Macho Sluts* by Pat Califia.

E) Who has the time to read!

F) *The Butter Battle Book* by Dr. Seuss.

8) Heroine

A) Dr. Penelope Leach, Child development specialist

B) She has a grudging respect for Jacqueline Onassis.

C) Gertrude Stein and Alice B. Toklas

D) Malcolm Forbes

E) Susie Bright, publisher of *On Our Backs*

F) The Cosmo Dyke and Emma Goldman

9) Social Groups

A) Any meeting where politically correct daycare is provided.

B) She has a membership in Gay Professional Women but can't seem to fit the events into her busy schedule. Being too busy to date in person she corresponds with other lesbians by writing letters to personals in gay computer bulletin boards.

C) Radical political groups on campus, any and all gay organizations. Currently applying for a ACLU card.

D) They are their own social group.

E) She is involved with any group where she might meet other lesbians of the same persuasion such as Dildos Anonymous, or Leather and Lace.

F) Her weekly Model Mugging Class, and continuing education classes in gourmet cooking.

Dinner Party Solution page 113

Across

3. needed a room of her own
7. a kind of clay
8. What Artemisia Gentileschi did
9. the runners were done in
10. first name of early American preacher
11. Bridget of Ireland was one
13. abrv. after the death
14. Judy Chicago's medium
16. Caroline Herschel, a ___ of the stars
19. symbolizes female as devourer/destroyer
20. Judith, a ___ heroine
22. to touch
23. the place where it occurred
24. a warrior woman
28. Theodora, Byzantine ___
30. could happen to a plate in the process of firing
31. Christine ___ Pisan, French author
36. British warrior queen
37. what happened to the earth during the ice age
38. an aid in remembering
39. makes it necessary to remake the plate
40. Ethel Smyth, ___ composer
43. Elizabeth R, queen of the English ___
44. Italian Gynecologist d. 1097
46. Sacajawea's role
48. of or like an old woman
50. Medieval religious figure, ___ of Bingen

Down

1. goes through a needle
2. what plates were decorated with
3. what the ancient women had
4. Mary Wollstonecraft wrote, A Vindication of the Rights ___ Woman
5. Dutch genius ___ van Schurman
6. nationality of Aspasia, scholar and philosopher
8. delicate clay
11. major contributor to women's birth control choices
12. the foundation
15. goddess who gives and takes life
16. Hrosvitha, a German ___
17. the nationality of Hypatia, a scholar and philosopher
18. holy wise woman
20. a green colored glaze
21. Egyptian Pharaoh
25. put the essence of 'woman' in her art
26. Renaissance noblewoman ___ d'Este
27. leading figure in Seneca Falls convention
29. what happened to Petronilla de Meath, for witchcraft
32. created the first convent
33. orange vegetable
34. spiritual tribe of native americans
35. Elizabeth Blackwell, founded ___ school for women
36. independent, extravagant lesbian
41. comes in when you're six years old
42. Eleanor of Aquitaine established the Courts of
45. Sojourner Truth, abolitionist ___ feminist
47. for example
49. same as #47 down

63

Watch Out Boys Solution page 113

Across

6. exist
8. they won't stand for that shit any longer
11. a printers measure
12. can be very annoying
13. green and sour
14. what women want
16. she was burned for wearing men's clothing
17. one
18. different
19. men that we don't like and on the bottom of shoes
21. women who betray-from the WW1 spy
22. it can be emotional as well as physical
23. slang for winning (two words)
24. one reason for machismo
26. what men sometimes don't want women to be
29. give a speech
31. what women are, traditionally, not expected to be
32. what women who won't conform are sometimes labeled
37. not under
38. another lousy man
39. singer from the '50's
40. because it was sci fi, gun-toting women didn't threaten men (movie)
43. traditonal men wear them
44. lines (abbrev.)
45. 'From Here ... Eternity'
47. watch out here we come
51. what a woman is not supposed to have done with a man
55. many men and some women still have trouble with this
56. Does he stand a chance?
57. not afraid to play a strong woman (first name)

Down

1. the guy you used to want to marry
2. watch out, we may bite
3. an outlawed insecticide
4. led her army against the invading Gauls
5. There were thirteen
6. an outlaw as feared as Billy the Kid
7. a witch's warning
8. a kind of dancing
9. can carry many times its own weight
10. what men never want to hear
11. deball
15. which (Latin)
18. a mouth or opening
20. a chinese measure
21. equality is one
25. some women regard traditional roles as one of these
27. what women don't want done to them
28. a railway in Chicago
30. toward
33. where your sex drive resides
34. 'A Question of....' (Dutch movie)
35. ....from grace
36. what pigs eat
41. an atheists wish
42. a term for the feminism of the 70s
46. last name of # 57 across
48. she didn't want a revolution if she couldn't dance
49. what women feel when they are not treated right
50. women's recourse to right injustice
52. what metal comes from
53. which came first
54. enchanted

Literary Women Solution page 113

Across

1. #38 down in the 1920's
5. destroyed by many lesbians
8. Lesbians Interested in Politics and Socializing (an accronym)
10. responsible for creating books
12. Down Lavender ...
14. Jo is the main one in 'Little Women'
17. What you'd like to write to your lover
18. considered first woman writer, British

Down

1. postal abbrv. for Guam
2. eager, willing and ...
3. Modern Language Association (abrv.)
4. to put into service
5. a figure of speech
6. what you stammer when at a loss for erotic words
7. what lesbians usually do better than men
8. Dickinson's attire
9. "We Outgrow Love Like Other Things," by Emily Dickinson

Across

19. a first edition of 'The Well of Lonliness'
21. to dine
23. to fasten, to bind
24. Holden Caulfield was the main character in this novel (last word)
26. indicated disbelief
27. a lesbian legend
29. Emily's forte
31. wrote ' A Member of the Wedding'
32. the famous Lisa
34. a word often used in romantic poetry
39. "___ Down the Walls"
40. lover of Virginia Woolf
45. name of a lesbian feminist press
46. good to suck on
47. very female fruit
48. a tool for weeding
49. a very caring person (abbrev.)
50. lesbian poet who didn't keep secret or silent

52. Cigar smoking poet
53. Did she really mean a cow?
57. 'The Voyage ___,' Virginia Woolf
58. wrote 'Silas Marner'
59. 'knew' both Henry and his wife
61. Woolf requirement
63. new and unusual, or long and verbose
65. Beauty and the ___
67. what the author weaves
70. here the words are sung
71. author of 'Pride and Prejudice,' init.
73. to do #23 across again
74. flowers for cunts
77. medieval medicine
78. "I meant to find her when I ___", Emily Dickinson

Down

10. what you do in order to meet the woman of your dreams
11. pen and ___
13. why some gay men and lesbians get dolled up
14. wrote about the pioneering, frontier spirit
15. Egyptian sun god
16. solo vocal with accompaniment
20. "Leave the ___ til we're dead," Virginia Woolf
21. 'A ___ in the House of Love,' Anais Nin
22. Stein's "The Mother of ___ All"
24. author of 'Goblin Market'
25. 'You' in the 17th Century
28. use this when you have to be straight forward
30. ran off with her lover and left their husbands at home
33. "Shouldn't be supported by federal funds" - Helms

34. small word for a sexual event
35. where the famous kiss between Abby and CJ took place (abrev.)
36. wrote about the importance of pockets
37. wrote 'Garden Party'and was envied by Virginia Woolf
38. what you couldn't show in the 1890's
41. image you try to project on 1st date
42. backbone of a ship
43. less than honest
44. wrote under a masculine pseudonym
49. what you don't want to get into with your lover
51. attended Natalie Barney's Thursday salons
53. 'The Little ___ and other stories,' Katherine Mansfield
54. Nefertiti's wasn't as elaborate as Tutakhamen's
55. an action to mislead
56. without cowboy boots
60. short love letters
62. muck
64. an extended narrative poem
66. ... and all
68. to feel ill
69. Hawaiian necklace
70. to damage
71. goes well with muffins
72. not a deterrent to good sex
75. Chinese word for horse
76. concerning

Film Solution page 113

Across

2. Eve Arden, among others, was a great one
5. life of Gertrude and Alice B. 'Waiting for the ___' 1987
8. the crew
10. story of Nin in 'Henry and ___' 1990
11. has and uses influence
16. an article
18. a swedish queen about whom a movie was made

Down

1. alternating current
2. to be there
3. a particular one
4. slang for tv
5. 'I've Heard the ___ Singing' 1987
6. Tuned In, Turned ---
7. to yearn painfully
9. network
11. Barbara Stanwyck as a New Orleans madam in 'Walk on the ___ Side' 1962

Across

20. '__ in Uniform' German Silent film 1931
23. noise in a movie starring Ingrid Bergman
25. indicates all
27. a detection system that uses sound waves
28. cupids arrow
29. psalm-singing lesbian spinster in 'Rachel, Rachel' __ Parsons 1968
31. a cheer
32. good love scenes inspire these
33. a women's jazz group
36. lesbians on a Canadian chicken farm in 'The __' 1968
39. she looked intensely
40. 'The __ of Sister George' 1968
43. Stein appears again in 'The __' 1987
44. an adversary
45. Candice Bergen as Lakey in Mary McCarthy's 'The __' 1968
47. funny hitchhiking lesbian ecology freaks in 'Five __ Pieces' 1970
49. to satisfy
52. one
53. always
56. first explicitly drawn lesbian character 1929 'Pandora's __'
57. June Allyson as a killer dyke in 'They Only Kill Their __' 1972
59. preposition for enclosed
61. popcorn's gone
62. ending of the Children's Hour
63. John Sayles' movie about lesbianism
64. abbr. for a state that is really homophobic
65. lesbians in athletics -1982 movie (second word)
66. symbol for the element nickel
67. exposing gays
69. 'Therese and Isabelle' the __ classic 1968
72. love in Reno, '__ Hearts' 1986
74. a kind of desire
75. "____ Guitar "-a movie with Mercedes McCambridge and Joan Crawford

Down

12. and
13. movie of lesbians in a mental hospital, 1964
14. a building block of life
15. a river in Poland
16. a widow continues her husband's affair in 'Richard's __' 1981
17. post-war France sets the stage for Miou Miou and Isabelle Huppert in __
19. second word of a well known play by Lillian Hellman
21. Patty Duke in 'By __', a lesbian couple wants a baby
22. good energy coming out
24. Honor Blackman as Pussy Galore in James Bond's '__' 1964
26. not you
29. used to form verbs indicating frequent or recurring action
30. to speak
34. brought movies into our living rooms
35. a poetic island
37. an award
38. lesbian passion in slow motion, Ingmar Bergman's '__' 1966
41. conjunction meaning possibly
42. Jane Alexander and Gena Rowlands in 'A Question of __' 1978
45. small winged insect that bites
46. a happy well-integrated lesbian couple in 'A __ Couple' 1979
48. observing
50. to get rid of
51. rare
52. very surprised
54. road in Sophia Loren's classic movie, 'Two Women'
55. usually not happy for the lesbian character
58. most movies reveal society's _____
60. positive lesbian love '__ Is Not Enough' 1975
62. a gay man and a lesbian fall in love, 'A Different __' 1980
64. state of being single
68. a bad movie starring Bo Derek
70. length of time for a movie or play
71. sung by Julie Andrews
73. star of 'Sylvia Scarlett' init.

CROSSWORD PUZZLE # 5

Signs   Solution page 113

Across

- 4. seed
- 7. forward
- 9. when the spirits come out to celebrate (3 words)
- 11. legendary ancient sorceresses
- 12. a witch's familiar
- 13. a novice or apprentice

Down

- 1. plump ones indicate sensual appetites
- 2. to partition
- 3. should never be loaned to a teammate
- 4. the tail is used in making potions
- 5. ultraviolet (abbrev.)

Across

16. an unlucky day
17. she brings good luck if she lights on your hand
19. to stitch
22. an army of women cannot
23. necessary for American women
24. protects you from sorcery
26. the female principle
27. ancient beverage still enjoyed today
28. Japanese spiritual practice
32. a woman who can see the future
34. a person's soul
36. to bother
37. spitting on it causes it to disappear
38. from whence all life springs
39. Sappho lived on one (French)
40. with style
42. head of state in moslem countries (alternate spelling)
43. if it falls, it brings bad luck
44. famous opera
45. the basis from which the rest grows
46. what wiccans are connected to
48. a label used for unconventional women
51. abbr. for a particular government organization
54. a preposition
55. a center of witchphobia
56. "--we meet again"
58. meditation will bring you to this state
60. a small portion
62. yields luscious purple fruit
63. "Fire and ___"
64. encircles the castle
65. member of an ascetic Jewish sect
66. "----, cats, sacks and wives"
67. land of the origin of the sun

Down

6. women together
8. the best butter is made during it
9. native Americans made food from these
10. where the water swirls
11. early American instrument
14. grain used to make intoxicating beverage
15. a pang of conscience
17. a Chinese measure of distance
18. some women need this support
20. the better to see you with
21. not always the goal
24. to absorb solar rays
25. brings sterility to anyone who touches it
28. well-known feminist spiritualist
29. lens opening
30. when they fly close to the ground, rain is on the way
31. one or two will bring death to chickens and ducks
33. said to cure asthma
35. politically correct pronoun
41. Egyptian god
45. the second command at the beginning of a race
47. evidence of past rites
48. the official association of witches
49. Ophelia's love
50. spilling it means a quarrel with a friend
52. a strong woman
53. Where Miss Jean Brodie always was
57. a sacred bird
59. to seriously surprise
61. where the ball is placed

Talk of the Town

The object of this game is to unscramble each word, then fit the letters on the crossword. One letter is common to both words; that letter has already been placed. The puzzles become progressively harder as more words are added. All the words in this round are distinctly part of the lesbian vernacular. As an example, the first one has been done . Solutions on page 113

All the help you can get

URPOPST ORUPG
SUPPORT GROUP

They said it couldn't be dcne

 # 1 SLNABEI OTRESHM

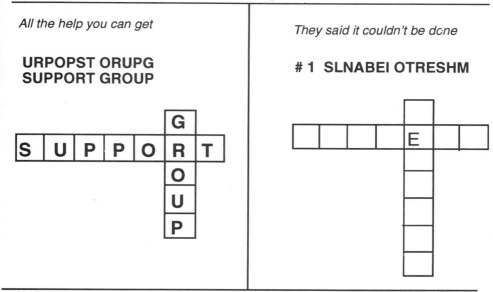

 # 2 FISINTEM TVEMONME
ATOLSENLW TSIOR

Shape our lives

Talk of the Town

Solution page 113

**# 3 SLOPECU TYREHAP
LLLCTPOYIAI RETCCOR**

The right thing to do

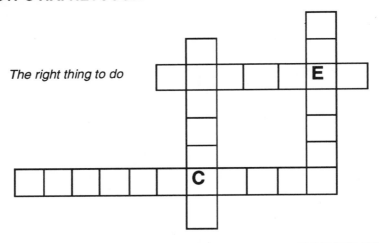

Solution page 113

**#4 IMSUC   ETVASILF
IESBALN ORIIBNLTEA
OMGINC TOU**

Makes you feel good

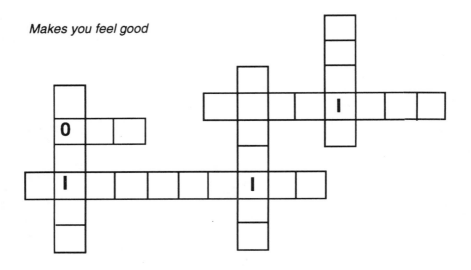

Solution page 114

Scenes of a Revolution

**#5 AONMW EIIEITDDNF
EUOTCRN RUUCETL
NBEAISL NNDDEROUGRU**

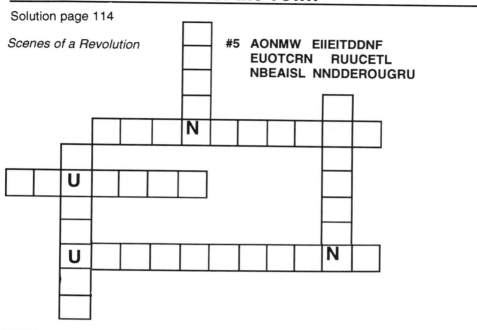

Don't just talk about it..

Solution page 114

**#6 DURTPCO TYTCOOB
ICAIPOLTL TAONIC
HCTELAI TTNNSSEIEMV
PIDER HRMCA**

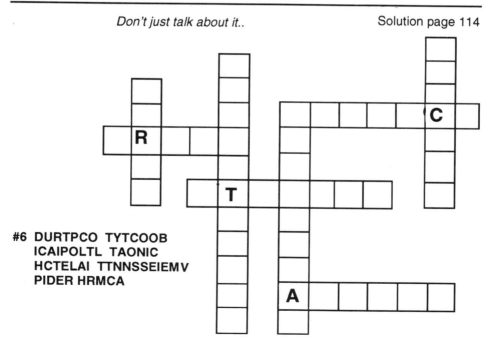

Talk of the Town —Trail Blazers

This final puzzle contains nine names of women noted for being leaders in their fields. Solution page 114

7
OARS KAPRS
RAGREATM DMAE
AEORELN VSLOROETE
RAPOH YRIENWF
LHISYER HHLOMISC

NANEOJ UOLLNA
RRAABBA NRODJA
LBAEL ZAGBU
TGREAARM RSAEGN

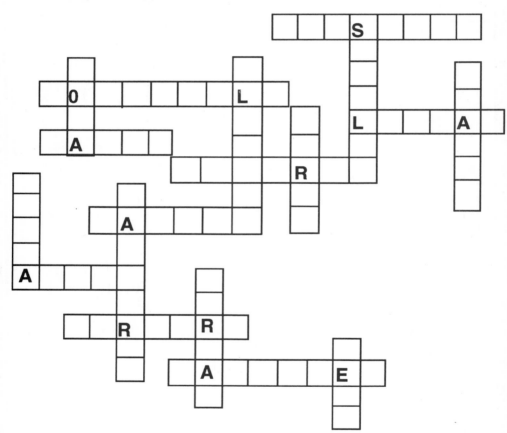

MATCH-UP #1

Solution page 115

UNDERSTANDING A THERAPIST'S LINGO
Select statements from the list below to match the appropriate therapist's statement.

What the therapist says....

How did that make you feel?

How long have you been having these thoughts?

Let's role play that situation.

It's important for you to learn how to let go.

It's fine to express your anger.

Excuse me while I take this telephone call.

Thank you for sharing.

Let's discuss my fee.

What the therapist means...

Our time is up.

Just how many personalities do you have?

Let me hear all your inner hostility.

Yikes! She's certainly pissed off.

I may have to refer her to a psychoanalyst.

What price do you place on your sanity?

Yippee! Another crisis!

Chill Out.

MATCH-UP #2

Solution page 115

YOUR PARENTS AND YOUR LIFESTYLE
Select from the list of statements below to match the appropriate translation of the parental statement.

What your parents say...

It would be nice if you dressed up this Christmas.

Is *she* coming home with you?

That hairstyle isn't my favorite.

How many holes do you have in your ear?

Have you ever met your cousin Arthur's best friend?

You two are welcome to sleep in the guest room.

Why don't you talk about the weather or something else?

We just want you to be happy.

What your parents mean....

Heavens! What will your relatives think when they see better decorations on your ears than on our Christmas tree!

Whatever you do, don't mention the 'L' word.

Are you still involved with a woman?

Twin beds will keep you apart!

We just want you to be straight.

Why don't you give a man a try?

Could you wear something other than jeans and a t-shirt?

You look like an army sergeant.

MATCH-UP #3

Solution page 115

YOU AND YOUR LOVER

What your lover says...

Love means never having to say you're sorry.

I'm not afraid of a commitment.

Nothing happened with her.

Maybe we should spend some time apart.

She's just a friend.

Believe me, there's no one else who interests me.

There are so many things about you that I love.

Of course what you do is important to me.

I have a headache.

What your lover means...

There are a million things you do that drive me nuts.

I hope you're not suggesting we move in together

She wants to sleep with me.

Please be a love and bring me two aspirin, massage my neck for awhile, kiss my shoulders, lick my naked back, and then make wild, passionate love to me for hours.

I haven't looked around in four days.

If you think I'm apologizing, you're wrong!

Aren't twelve arguments in two hours a personal record for us?

Tell me about your day after *L.A. Law* .

I stopped myself just short of orgasm.

MATCH-UP #4

BAR PICK-UP LINES
Select from the list of statements below to match the appropriate translation of the pick-up line.

What you hear...

Come here often?

I don't usually ask anyone to dance.

So what do you do for work?

Are those your friends you're with?

Can I buy you a drink?

Crowded, isn't it?

I like that shirt.

You're a really fascinating lady.

I'd really like to get to know you.

What it means...

Are you rich?

I have a half hour 'til last call to try to score with you.

I haven't been able to figure out what to do on the dance floor since disco died.

I can't stop rubbing my body against yours.

My lover and I just split up and I haven't seen the inside of a bar for the past five years.

I guess I'll hang out with you until I get bored.

Let's sleep together.

Is the diesel dyke with the knife in her back pocket your lover?

God, you have great cleavage!

78

MATCH-UP #5

Solution page 115

NANCY DREW MYSTERY STORIES

Here's Nancy Drew again, one of the few strong women models from our childhood. Use the list of clues and the story titles listed below to match the published title of the Nancy Drew mystery to its appropriate clue.

Clues	The story title
Hush-hush, antique tick-tick	The Hidden Window Mystery
Info in busted jewlery	The Clue in the Diary
Info in ancient pictures	The Ringmaster's Secret
Termite-phobic hush-hush woman	The Clue of the Leaning Chimney
Dorothy's puzzling footwear	The Ghost of Blackwood Hall
Can't find the pane puzzle	The Clue in the Old Album
Info from crooked smoker	The Mystery at the Ski Jump
Look for lost directions	The Quest of the Missing Map
Puzzle at house of plants	The Secret of the Old Clock
Airborn Rossinols puzzle	The Mystery at the Moss-Covered Mansion
Empty tree note	The Secret in the Old Attic
The meaning of weird wax	The Clue in the Jewel Box
Me and my out west hush-hush	The Secret at Shadow Ranch
Circular circus hush-hush	The Message in the Hollow Oak
Ebony unlockers info	The Secret of the Wooden Lady
Spectre in Blackwood corridor	The Clue of the Black Keys
Hush-hush under the elderly roof	The Scarlet Slipper Mystery
Info in precious metals container	The Sign of the Twisted Candles
Puzzle of the metal bonded elephant's nose	The Mystery of the Brass Bound Trunk
Info in journal	The Clue of the Broken Locket

MATCH-UP #6

Solution page 116

SOFTBALL ATHLETES' EXCUSES
Select from the list of statements below to match the appropriate softball excuse.

What they say...

The umping stank.

Their clean up batter takes steroids.

I can't stand their pitcher.

I had a good hit in the third inning.

Their playing field is a mess.

The people watching the game were really loud and obnoxious.

What they mean...

Their pitcher is my ex.

If they hadn't spent two hours lining the damn field, the fair ball wouldn't have been so obvious...

I was one for six at the plate.

We sucked.

At least they had fans...

Our cleanup batter can't hit out of the in-field.

MATCH-UP #7

Solution page 116

STATEMENTS FROM THE POLITICALLY INCORRECT
Select from the list of statements below to match the appropriate political sentiment.

What they say...

I really care what happens to dolphins.

I'm cutting down on meat.

Abused women need help.

I recycle.

Animals have rights too.

It's important to support lesbian businesses.

I support lesbian politicians.

What they mean...

I redeem my empties.

I drop ten bucks every Saturday night at the bar.

I won't do my imitation of Flipper again.

If she's cute, I'll vote for her.

I slow down every time I see a squirrel crossing the road.

I only eat two burgers instead of three.

Tomorrow I'm asking my boss for a raise.

#1 LESBIAN ANNIVERSARY GIFTS
Select items from the list of Lesbian Gifts below to match the appropriate anniversary year.

Year	Traditional Gift	Lesbian Gift
1st	Paper	A psychically in-tune quartz
2nd	Cotton	Gift certificate to a tanning salon
3rd	Leather	Subscription to a gay newspaper
4th	Fruit, flowers	An encyclopedia of precious stones and gems
5th	Wood	A take-out Chinese dinner
6th	Candy	A *Wizard of Oz* video
7th	Wool, copper	Statue of a Greek goddess
		A cord of split wood
8th	Bronze	An original recording by *Ruby and the Romantics*
9th	Pottery	Purchase of a softball field
10th	Tin	Lavendar silk sheets
11th	Steel	An autographed copy of Tracy Chapman's first gold album
12th	Silk	
13th	Lace	Earth-conscious paper bags to store recyclable tin cans
14th	Ivory	Leather dildo harness
15th	Crystal	A pair of silver earrings in the shape of handcuffs
20th	China	Black and Decker Skil Saw
25th	Silver	Rawhide shoe laces for work boots
30th	Pearl	Tofu chocolate
35th	Coral	Scuba diving equipment
40th	Ruby	Dedication of the softball field
45th	Sapphire	Passion fruit and ladyslippers
50th	Gold	A case of heavy-duty hand cleaner
55th	Emerald	T-shirt from the Michigan Women's Festival
60th	Diamond	L.L. Bean shirt, plaid, with a penny in each breast pocket
75th	Diamond	A copy of *Audubon's Guide to Seashells*

LEZ–TELL RECORDS presents

A collection of the best–loved Christmas carols, for lesbians, as sung by
RUBY & THE RED–NOSED REINDYKES.
*Invite the gang to sing along with these all–time favorites as they
decorate your artificial tree in front of the portable heater!*

DECK THE HALLS WITH BARB & HOLLY
I CAME AT MIDNIGHT WITH CLAIRE
FRANCIE THE SNOW–WOMAN
OH LITTLE BAR IN BOSTON–TOWN
HARK! IT'S HARRIET! MY HEART TAKES WING!
JINGLE EAR CUFFS
ANGELS WE HAVE HEARD WHILE HIGH
SILENT NIGHT (MY BABE'S NOT IN SIGHT)
SUZUKI SLEIGH RIDE
RUDY, THE RED–NOSED REINDYKE

And look for these other LES–TELL Record Collections:
LESBIAN RELIGIOUS HYMNS, performed by the San Francisco All–Girl Marching Band
BAR DRINKING SONGS, performed by the Clean & Sober Dykes
CAMPFIRE SONGS, performed by Wildwimmin of Vermont

"GREAT FIRST PAGES"

TITLE: _____

"Don't you think it's time to come inside the house, Jackie love? It's getting cool out and you're not wearing your sweater," Nadine said to her lover from behind the screen door. Jackie looked at Nadine from her seat on the porch, but couldn't see her very well; Nadine was just a fuzzy, out-of-focus body talking to her.

"I'll be in in a minute, dear," Jackie replied. "I want a few moments to appreciate the evening and the garden before the mosquitoes kick me out."

"Okay. I'll start dinner, then."

"Good. I'll be in soon to help you."

Nadine shut the inside door part-way to keep the cool evening air out and the warm kitchen air in. Jackie saw this and smiled, then looked out over their property at the lush green vegetables and colorful wildflowers. I couldn't be happier, she thought.

"But you haven't met Elsa," she heard a woman's soft, gentle voice speak in her mind.

"Huh?" she asked aloud. The birds stopped chirping, as if they were listening, too. "What did you say?" she asked, sitting up in her chair. She turned to the door, but the voice hadn't come from that direction.

She stood up and walked slowly down the stairs to the lawn, then walked across the lawn towards the vegetable garden. "Come to Elsa," the woman's voice whispered in her mind. Jackie stopped in her tracks. The voice had sounded closer, clearer. "Who are you?" she asked aloud. "Where are you?"

There was no reply. She resumed her walk towards the garden.

"Come to Elsa," the woman's voice again said aloud, as if she were standing in front of her.

Startled, she stopped and strained to see ahead of her in the dusky hue of evening.

Suddenly Jackie felt someone touch her right hand, grasp it, and pull it gently away from her body, as if leading her. Jackie tried to pull away, but the grasp tightened and held her hand firmly. "What's going on?" she asked aloud, trying to sound indignant but feeling only fear.

"Come to Elsa. She wants you," the voice replied.

"Who the hell is Elsa?" she asked as she tried, again unsuccessfully, to remove her hand from the unseen being's grasp.

"I am Elsa," she then heard.

"GREAT FIRST PAGES"

TITLE: _____

Detective M.J. Falcon of the Chicago Police Department surveyed the murder scene. The woman's body, that of famed lesbian author Katie Woods, was slumped over the keyboard of her word processor. The letter "I" had been repeated for approximately 150 pages before the notation had flashed on the screen, "This disk is almost full! Saving the material may free up space." The woman had never responded to the computer's suggestion. She had been dead, according to the coroner's estimate, by the time she had hit the first "I" six hours earlier.

"What else did you find out?" M.J.asked Carla, the county coroner.

"She died of a massive head wound. Something crushed the top of her skull."

M.J. stopped writing in her notepad for a moment. "What do you mean, something ?"

Carla shrugged her shoulders. "Just what I said. The top of her head has been crushed in a way that suggests a large piece of concrete fell on it. But she obviously didn't know someone was about to bop her off the top of her skull. The position of the wound is exactly at the top of her head, as if she was typing at the word processor and suddenly got hit from above."

"Like from the ceiling?" M.J. suggested as she looked up at the ornately scrolled ceiling in the author's study.

"Check. But you can see," Carla pointed out as she craned her neck to follow M.J.'s gaze, "that there's not even a small piece of plaster missing. The other odd thing," she continued as she tapped M.J.'s arm and walked over to the victim's chair, "is that there's a pool of water under her chair. Mixed with her blood, of course."

"Of course," M.J. nodded as she looked at the pale pink water.

"What I had thought at first," Carla said, "is a water leak in the ceiling had loosened a piece of plaster, which had then fallen on her. But…," Carla waved her arm around the crime scene, "…there's not a speck of plaster dust and the ceiling's intact. M.J., this babe got bopped from above. And she certainly wasn't expecting it."

"Okay, Carla, thanks. You'll keep me apprised of what your autopsy reveals, right?"

"But of course." Carla grinned, then gathered up her things. "I'm off."

M.J. stared at the body for several moments. Who killed Katie Woods, the most prolific, though certainly not the best, lesbian writer? What was the motive? How did she die?

"This may be my hardest case yet," M.J. said to herself.

"GREAT FIRST PAGES"

TITLE: _____

A dinner plate flew over Bobbie's head and smashed hard against the kitchen wall behind her, throwing fragments in all directions. "Shit, that was close!" Jennifer noted from her crouched position behind a chair in the dining room.

"See what I mean!" Bobbie cried out and ducked as another plate sailed in her direction and flew into wall.

"This happens every night?" Jennifer asked as she peered out from behind the chair.

"Every night for the past week," Bobbie said as she assumed a defensive stance, arms spread out and knees bent, rapidly looking in all directions in an effort to keep watch for the next piece of dinnerware. "Then, when I wake up in the morning, all the dishes are stacked just as they were in the cabinets. There's not even one chip on the floor."

"But I don't get it," Jennifer replied, then shouted, "Look out! The silverware drawer!"

Bobbie lunged to close the drawer that had been pulled open, but she was too late. The flatware rose up in a massive gray unit, hovered in the air for a moment, then, like a flying squadron of World War II fighter planes, sailed past her. Bobbie ducked.

"Watch out, Bobbie," Jennifer called out, then screamed as the airborn flatware headed in her direction. At that moment, the cuckoo clock voiced one hearty "cuckoo," and the flatware crashed harmlessly to the floor next to Jennifer.

"That should be it," Bobbie said as she sighed and relaxed her shoulders.

Jennifer stared at the flatware lying next to her.

"Yup, that's it," Bobbie confirmed as she crunched through the kitchen on fragments of broken dinnerware.

Jennifer slowly shook her head as she stood up and surveyed the destruction. "I don't get it. Every night, from midnight to 1 a.m., this happens? Then, when you wake up in the morning, you come downstairs and it's all cleaned up — and intact — as if nothing has happened?"

"That's part of it, yes," Bobbie replied. "What I didn't tell you is what happens in the bedroom from 2 to 3."

Jennifer smiled and took Bobbie's hand. "Oh, I know what happens then. That involves you and me, doesn't it Bobbie Boo?" she cooed in a playful voice.

Bobbie gave her a tired smile and squeezed her hand. "Well, Jen, it involves you, me, and a ghost."

Jennifer stepped back from her. "What?"

"Let me explain."

"GREAT FIRST PAGES"

TITLE: _____

"Hey, babe, come here often?"

Charlene coolly tapped her cigarette ashes into the ashtray on the bar counter. Then she shifted position on her bar stool slightly to assess the body that went along with the voice that had asked her the question.

A tall, dark-haired woman with broad shoulders, dark green eyes, and a shapely body met her gaze.

Charlene put the cigarette to her lips, slowly parted them, and lightly sucked on the cigarette. Then she took the cigarette away from her mouth and slowly licked her lips. She met the dark-haired woman's eyes. "I haven't come here at all," she replied as thin streams of smoke accompanied her words. "In fact, I don't come in bars."

The dark-haired woman grinned and tipped her head back to let out a quick laugh. Then she faced Charlene. "That's something we share in common, lady. We're off to a good start."

"Who says we've started anything?"

She grinned again. "Touché, lady cool. I guess with you, I shouldn't be so presumptuous. Tell me, then, have you got a name?"

"Since the day I was born," Charlene replied as she feigned interest in her drink.

The dark-haired woman sat down next to her and watched as Charlene ran a finger up and down the outside of the sweating cocktail glass. Then Charlene placed the moist finger tip in her mouth and sucked on it. She felt the dark-haired woman focus her gaze on what her mouth was doing to her finger.

"I've got something else you might like to suck on, lady."

Charlene met the dark-haired woman's eyes for a moment, then let her eyes drop to the woman's chest.

The dark-haired woman smiled. "There, yes. And other places, too."

Charlene sighed, picked up her drink, tipped her head back, and drained the cocktail. She placed the glass on the counter, then shook her head at the dark-haired woman. "Not interested."

"Oh, I beg to differ."

"Beg all you want. I'm a woman who doesn't change her mind."

"Well, tonight, lady cool, you will."

"What makes you so sure?"

"This," the dark-haired lady said.

Title: _____

Miriam flipped idly through the pages of the dog-eared women's magazine that looked like it had been thumbed through countless times; she glanced quickly at the cover of the magazine and located the publishing date — two years old. She tossed the magazine onto the low table in front of her, settled back in the hard chair, and crossed her legs.

"Miriam Stephens?" an attractive blonde in white called out, one eyebrow raised, as she opened the door to the waiting room and scanned the room looking at those who were waiting.

"That's me," Miriam replied as she stood. The woman gestured for Miriam to follow her through the door that led to the examining rooms. The blonde then opened a door with a large blue A on it to allow Miriam to enter the room first.

Then she closed the door behind them. "So how have you been feeling?" she asked as she beckoned Miriam to take a seat next to a table with a blood pressure cuff. When Miriam sat down, the blonde wrapped the cuff around Miriam's arm and pumped air into it. Miriam read her nameplate — Ginny Weirs, L.P.N., as Nurse Weirs listened to her stethoscope.

"Well, I seem to be having a…uh…slight problem," Miriam replied as she looked into the nurse's deep blue eyes.

"Oh? What's the problem?"

"Well, maybe I should show you." Miriam blushed. "I'm a little embarrassed about it."

Nurse Weirs smiled. "There's no need to be embarrassed. In this job, believe me, I've seen just about everything."

Miriam smiled for the first time in weeks. "Okay. That makes me feel better."

The nurse unwrapped the cuff from Miriam's arm. "Your blood pressure's great," she commented. "Now, why don't you take your clothes off, slip on the gown on the examining table, and we'll find out what's going on. I'll just step outside. Call me when you're ready."

Miriam nodded, then stripped when the nurse left the room. She pulled the gown on, then called out, "I'm set."

"Good," the nurse said as she came back into the room and closed the door. "Now, can you describe your problem to me?"

"I think it's better if I show you," Miriam replied as she dropped the gown to the floor and stood naked in front of the nurse.

"GREAT FIRST PAGES"

TITLE: _____

Stephanie was certain that it all began with the strawberries, although she couldn't say for sure. But the strawberries had been part of that strange day...

She had been at a friend's cookout that afternoon, enjoying the juicy hamburgers and tasty potato salad. After the main meal, Sarah — an attractive, successful lawyer who was new to town — had smiled invitingly at her as she had placed two oversized, strawberry-coated, oozingly inviting cheesecakes on the picnic table. Stephanie, as well as the others at the cookout, had helped herself not once, but twice to the dessert. The cheesecake was fluffy, not stuffy; the strawberries were ripe and juicy. Yum, yum, Stephanie had thought at the time.

But Stephanie didn't partake amply of the dessert just because it was delicious; she had also wanted to be able to strike up a conversation with Sarah and thought she could begin by personally complementing her on her cooking skills.

As Stephanie talked at length with the charming and eye-pleasing Sarah over cups of freshly brewed coffee, she realized that she had fallen deeply and hopelessly in love with her.

So, before she left the cookout, she had exchanged telephone numbers with Sarah, along with a promise to her call soon.

Two hours later, while Stephanie was home watching television with her cat, Samantha, happily settled on her food-rounded stomach, the sneezing began.

One sneeze, two sneezes, three sneezes in a row. The cat had leaped from her lap and crouched low as Stephanie raced by her to the bathroom for a tissue.

Four sneezes, five sneezes, six sneezes.

Blow, blow, blow.

"Yuck," she pronounced aloud. "I feel like hell. My eyes are puffy and red and tearing like crazy. And are they ever itchy!" She wanted to rub and rub and rub them.

"Oh, no," she said with dread as she reached for a tissue against the next sneeze advance.

"Two more sneezes and my brain will be blown to pee .... pee...to pee-seez!" Stephanie blew her now-aching nose and forced her puffy eyes open to survey herself in the mirror.

She couldn't believe what she saw.

"GREAT FIRST PAGES"

TITLE: _____

I am a marathoner.

I like the feel of the road beneath me, its special scars and weathered surface, grooved and gravelly, pock- marked and scabbed as the knees of a rugby player.

I like the course of the road, its steady flow towards a destination despite twists and turns past shelters erected along its banks of sidewalks.

The road is my life-giving river. I skim upon its hard surface, swimming in sweat, plunging within myself to find the strength, time and time again, to forge against its powerful current like a salmon struggling upstream.

I have learned much from the road. It has been a savage teacher, cruelly robbing me of my innocence; it has been a powerful rebuilder, patiently restoring my courage.

I love being a marathoner, but some say I am not a runner in the true sense of the word. Because I am in a wheelchair, some see me not as an athlete but as an aberration.

To those people I say, "I was born an athlete and I will die an athlete. I run with my mind; my body is merely the vehicle. Together, we are tuned to my visions of victory."

Like the time I ran the Boston Marathon...

I perform my pre-race ritual. Like a race car driver revving up for the track, I check my equipment. I push off on a short sprint through the warm-up area, throw on my brakes in a sudden stop, make some adjustments, then short-sprint back down. I rub nuts and bolts with a cloth as if I am kneading my joints; I oil cogs and wires as if I am pumping blood into my veins and arteries. I lace my legs tightly to the metal supports. I lift myself and shift positions until I am settled comfortably in the seat. Then I stretch my arms and wave them above me, around me, in front of me, taking care that my shirt and shorts do not restrict any of my movements.

The fine-tuning complete, I roll away from the crowd and lock my brakes some distance from them. I quiet my mind and listen to the positive messages I give myself: I have trained for today's marathon — swimming, weight lifting, and "running" long, winding roads. I am in top physical shape. I will win this race. I am swifter. I am stronger.

I am the best.

I move my wheelchair into position at the starting line.

PUSSYPOP

The Microwavable Popcorn with kernels that pop in the shape of a labia!

Try the buttery *Movie-style* – a finger–licking good popcorn flavored with imitation dairy butter from an imitation dairy cow.

Or try the *Chedda Chompa* – the Boston favorite – with a snappy blend of herbs and spices and enough tropical oils to send your cholesterol levels through the roof.

Then there's the *Yum-Yup* – the pricey popcorn for the lesbian yuppie on the go, coated with rich Godiva chocolate and sprinkled liberally with macadamia nuts, guaranteed not to soil expensive BMW leather.

Or stick with *Crunchy Original* – your basic, conservative, salted, oiled, greased–&–ready–to–kick–ass style popcorn that rivals Newman's Own, yet contributes to no charitable causes.

PUSSYPOP
The kernal you can't wait to get in your mouth!

Building Blocks Example—Looking For A Cure.

The object of this game is to complete each word that is listed horizontally by filling in the empty block. All the words in the puzzle share a common theme and the empty block will reveal the theme. Words can be any length and there are more letters per line than are used in each word. The first one shows you how it's done. Solution page 116

S	G	A	R	M	A	S	H	A	M	A	N	S	T
U	D	U	N	U	R	S	E	S	U	S	H	E	S
U	G	O	T	A	V	F	A	I	T	H	I	N	A
P	L	K	E	L	F	O	L	K	L	O	R	E	K
S	M	I	D	W	I	V	E	S	I	N	G	L	Y
T	D	D	K	L	E	C	R	O	N	E	S	E	S
P	D	O	C	T	O	R	S	P	R	O	C	T	R

Building Blocks #1   SayWhat?

Solution page 116

R	O	V	E	R	B	A		O	L	Y	O	N	L	Y
D	E	A	R	N	H	E		R	I	N	G	I	N	G
I	M	O	N	S	I	G		S	V	R	E	S	T	R
A	L	H	E	I	R	O		L	Y	P	H	S	S	I
D	N	T	C	O	M	M		N	I	C	A	T	E	E
H	A	I	L	A	B	R		I	L	L	E	D	E	R
N	U	N	V	R	B	L		E	S	T	U	R	E	S
V	E	R	C	O	N	V		R	S	A	T	I	O	N

Building Blocks #2 Praise Be

Solution page 116

O	G	O	D	D	E		S	I	N	H	I	S	E
A	L	I	N	A	S		R	A	Y	E	R	O	H
S	T	I	K	A	W		C	C	A	D	A	Y	R
I	W	A	N	T	A		O	T	C	A	K	K	E
M	Y	S	T	I	C		S	M	Y	S	C	E	T
M	E	D	I	T	A		I	O	N	A	T	O	N
A	N	T	N	A	T		R	E	C	A	L	S	U
V	C	T	V	C	H		N	N	E	L	I	N	G
R	E	W	O	R	E		I	G	I	O	N	L	Y
M	A	S	C	E	T		C	I	S	M	Y	S	T
A	S	S	A	I	N		S	C	O	M	A	R	C
H	I	R	H	O	L		Y	R	O	L	Y	N	G

Building Blocks #3 Let's Talk

Solution page 116

O	U	B	L	O	O	P	E	O		O	U	P	L	E	S	E	T
L	U	F	A	K	E	C	O	N		M	I	C	O	M	I	C	O
G	R	O	W	L	O	G	R	O		P	I	N	L	Y	G	R	E
O	C	C	U	P	A	T	I	O		A	L	N	A	T	A	N	C
T	E	X	C	E	P	R	E	X		E	X	Y	U	A	L	L	M
H	A	R	D	A	R	C	A	R		E	R	C	L	F	E	A	V
P	O	O	H	S	C	H	O	O		S	O	S	H	A	L	P	T
M	O	D	A	M	R	F	A	M		L	Y	D	I	S	F	N	J
I	N	C	I	D	E	I	N	I		D	I	V	I	D	U	A	L
W	H	I	M	A	R	R	I	A		E	A	V	E	R	G	O	W

Building Blocks #4 — Don't Assume

Solution page 116

```
B  L  O  C  L  A  S  │    │  I  S  M  L  E  S  E
F  A  K  B  E  A  U  │    │  Y  I  S  K  I  M  D
W  I  T  I  D  I  V  │    │  R  S  I  T  Y  G  R
C  V  D  I  F  F  E  │    │  E  N  C  E  S  A  N
X  C  E  G  E  N  D  │    │  R  I  N  R  A  L  L
R  D  A  R  C  A  R  │    │  L  E  S  P  L  A  A
O  H  O  R  O  F  S  │    │  I  G  M  A  S  L  P
M  A  J  O  R  I  T  │    │  L  Y  Y  U  L  E  S
C  I  D  E  S  T  E  │    │  M  O  T  H  E  R  S
I  M  A  S  T  R  A  │    │  G  H  T  S  U  G  O
M  S  T  X  S  T  N  │    │  A  M  E  S  H  R  T
S  N  U  M  E  R  A  │    │  E  I  S  M  M  L  Y
```

Building Blocks #5 — Women's Work

Solution page 116

```
N  U  M  R  O  N  O  │    │  I  R  S  T  L  A  D  Y
E  R  K  C  E  C  L  │    │  R  K  S  K  E  A  E  R
O  L  E  D  O  L  I  │    │  O  D  E  L  S  L  A  M
D  I  E  T  I  C  I  │    │  N  S  N  A  T  A  N  S
L  I  B  R  A  T  E  │    │  I  B  R  A  R  I  A  N
E  R  A  H  I  N  H  │    │  A  L  E  R  S  E  A  R
```

93

Building Blocks Women's Work cont.

Solution page116

N	T	U	N	A	G	E		S	H	A	S	G	R	L	S
P	E	E	N	S	T	E		O	G	R	A	P	H	E	R
G	H	O	T	E	L	R		E	L	L	E	R	T	E	R
K	B	O	O	K	K	E		P	E	R	S	P	E	R	A
C	I	D	E	A	G	E		T	S	N	U	T	T	S	N
A	M	A	S	S	E	U		E	S	U	E	S	S	E	S
P	O	P	R	O	S	T		T	U	T	E	S	E	D	Y
C	C	A	R	E	G	I		E	R	S	A	N	T	K	R
C	R	E	A	R	E	C		P	T	I	O	N	I	S	T

Women's Work Cont.

Solution page 116

G	O	O	C	S	O	C		O	K	S	P	O	O	S	K
M	E	D	I	E	D	U		A	T	O	R	S	T	A	L
R	E	C	R	E	S	E		R	E	T	A	R	I	E	S
N	U	M	U	V	O	L		N	T	E	E	R	S	T	Y
A	L	S	T	R	I	P		E	R	S	O	M	A	L	S
N	O	H	O	M	E	M		K	E	R	S	I	N	L	Y
U	N	N	U	T	R	I		I	O	N	I	S	T	E	D
Y	P	P	S	Y	C	H		C	S	M	Y	S	M	T	Y
C	O	U	N	S	E	L		R	S	I	M	D	H	L	P
S	T	R	U	N	N	U		S	B	U	L	M	D	U	L
P	E	R	E	S	T	E		E	E	R	S	R	E	E	R

You know the Romance is gone but the love remains when...

... Instead of dining by candlelight, you eat supper in front of the T.V. together.

...going to bed means going to sleep.

...instead of lighting a fire in the fireplace, you plug in the space heater.

...you start using abbreviations for the pet names you call each other.

...instead of bringing home flowers, you bring home toilet paper.

...you put lotion on her back to help relieve her dry skin.

...you take midnight strolls together to burn off dinner.

....you use vacation time together to catch up on your yardwork.

...you take out Chinese instead of making gourmet food for each other.

...you meet her family.

...you don't have to explain anything.

Cosmodyke

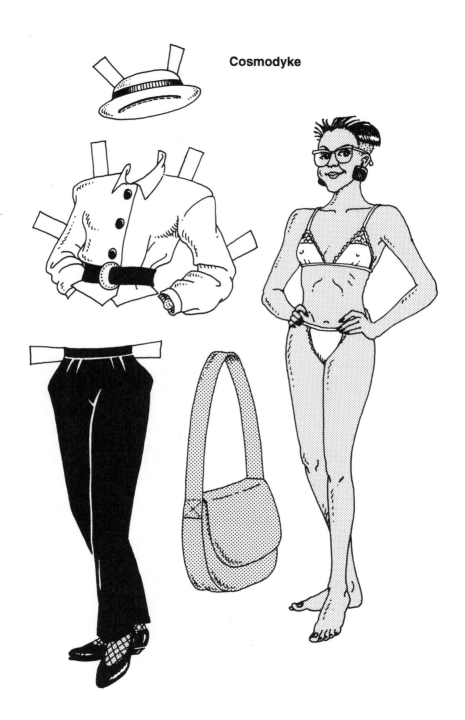

1) Identification A) Cosmodyke

2) Description

D) This is a Lesbian version of the Charlie Girl, a sophisticated woman-about-town who knows what she wants and how to get it. Whatever is currently in vogue, she is into. She dresses in the height of fashion with such confidence and style that she can get away with wearing clothes which on another woman would actually look ugly. Only Astor Place (the birth place of American punk haircuts) will suffice for her ultra-short haircut. This is the type of woman who literally wouldn't be caught dead in Birkenstocks. Even seeing people wearing them, especially with socks, makes her nauseous.

3) Accoutrements

A) Everything vital for life survival in the big city can be found in the large leather shoulder bag she carries everywhere—books, cosmetics, bus tokens, underwear, clothing changes, a toothbrush—anything that she may need at any time of the day, the night or possibly the next morning.

4) Habitat

E) The chic shopping centers in any city in the U.S. or abroad. She is usually seen at the theater, outdoor cafes, foreign film theaters and in line for the Mapplethorpe exhibit.

5) Transportation

E) She knows how to get to Hawaii and back on public transportation.

6) Common Expressions

C) "Damn, I missed my bus!" " Yo taxi."

7) Last Book Read

C) Whatever is number one on the New York Times best seller list.

8) Heroine

B) She has a grudging respect for Jacqueline Onassis.

9) Social Groups

F) Her weekly Model Mugging Class, and continuing education classes in gourmet cooking.

Campus Dyke

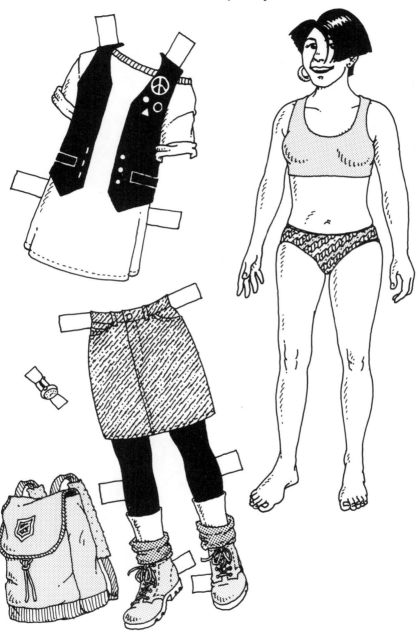

CONNECT THE DYKES ANSWERS

1) Identification B) Campus Dyke

2) Description

E) This intense young woman has a fairly distinct style. Her haircut is always on the cutting edge of fashion in some type of dramatic schizophrenic affair. Her clothing follows suit—oversized men's shirts with skin tight mini skirts. She wants to be announced before she enters a room and she accomplishes this by her appearance. This sense of the dramatic is evident in her life. When she is involved in something, her participation is complete and passionate. She not only cares for the whales, (porpoises, animal, people, etc, but she insists that everyone else should care as well.

3) Accoutrements

F) This is a person who loves to accessorize with large jewelry. Her watch is huge—at least one wrist is covered with bangle bracelets. Her earrings seem to follow the same two-toned effect as her haircut with exceedingly large earrings in one side and small studs or crystals in the other. Over her shoulder she carries the required large leather knapsack stuffed to the gills with text books, note paper, CDs with a portable player, and the latest issue of *Premier* magazine.

4) Habitat

B) Found either singly or in groups, on college campuses everywhere. She may physically be in a small state college in rural Tennessee, but in her heart and attitude she is in downtown Boston or San Francisco.

5) Transportation

D) If she is anywhere near a city she is completely at home using any type of public transportation. If she can afford to own a car it is most likely a recently repainted, beat up old VW bug.

6) Common Expressions

E) "But if you only understood the plight of_____ you would agree with me!"

7) Last Book Read

B) *Pure Lust* by Mary Daly

8) Heroine

F) The Cosmodyke and Emma Goldman

9) Social Groups

C) Radical political groups on campus, any and all gay organizations, Currently applying for a ACLU card.

Fused Couple

101

1) Identification— E) Fused Couple

2) Description

B) There may be a wide variation in appearance, but the members of each set resemble each other. This resemblance tends to increase as the relationship develops. They have identical haircuts, identical clothes (in fact problems may arise when they can't remember whose clothes are whose) identical jewelry (given lovingly to each other), etc. The strong resemblance between these two lesbians often causes straight people to ask, "Are you two sisters?"

3) Accoutrements

D) Accoutrements may vary from couple to couple, but internally are the same. Identical knapsacks, identical softball gloves—even identical pets!

4) Habitat

C) May be found anywhere: grocery stores, concerts, campgrounds. Whenever you find one, the other isn't far away.

5) Transportation

F) This is the one area in which they differ. Because they are actually two people (although discerning this may be difficult at times), their vehicles vary for practical reasons. For example one may own a sports car (that seats two) for going out and looking cool, while the other may have a pickup truck with bucket seats for transporting a rototiller or going to the dump—and looking cool. But whichever vehicle one is driving, the other usually goes along.

6) Common Expressions

B) This is a literal term for the these lesbian who are known for finishing each others sentences. They tend to speak in unison.

7) Last Book Read

A) Aloud together—*Lesbian Couples* by D. Merille Lunis and G. Dorsey Green.

8) Heroine

C) Gertrude Stein and Alice B. Toklas

9) Social Groups

D) They are their own social group.

Leather Dyke

1) Identification   D) Leather Dyke

2) Description

A) This woman may look a little scary. Her outfit may consist of a leather vest with nothing on underneath it and skin tight leather pants, or maybe chaps over jeans with a red handkerchief protruding from the left rear pocket. On her feet are blunt-toed or silver tipped black 'fuck you' boots. She may also adorn herself with a silver studded black leather belt and bracelet (maybe even a collar). Her hair is cropped short and she wears a Muir cap set at a rakish angle. Tiny silver handcuffs are earring possibilities and she has at least one tattoo.

3) Accoutrements

E) This lesbian realizes the importance of accessorizing. She usually has a variety of sex aids readily available: silk ties, nipple clamps, handcuffs, leather straps and dildoes.

4) Habitat

F) She can be found hanging out at any gay bar with pool tables and more than one motorcycle parked outside, or at head shops that feature sex toys.

5) Transportation

A) A motorcycle (not less than five hundred c.c.s) preferably a Harley

6) Common Expressions

F) "Top or bottom?"

7) Last Book Read

D) *Macho Sluts* by Pat Califia.

8) Heroine

E)Susie Bright, publisher of *On Our Backs.*

9) Social Groups

E) She is involved with any group where she might meet other lesbians of the same persuasion such as Dildos Anonymous or Leather and Lace.

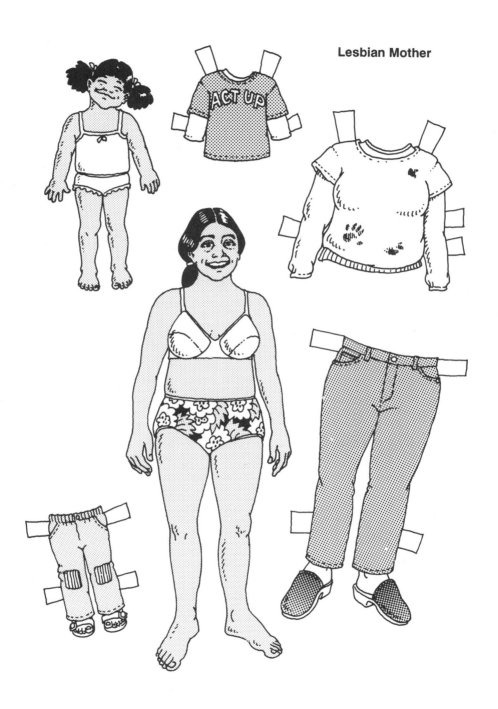

Lesbian Mother

1) Identification F) Lesbian Mother

2) Description

C) After much research, debate, time and money this lesbian finally became pregnant through artificial insemination. Having a child in her life is not only a personal satisfaction, but is also a political statement. She knew what would be involved to enroll her child in school and dealing with her family members and other parents at the PTA. But she may not have been prepared for the pure physical exhaustion a little dyke-tyke came with. She is often easy to recognize by her exhausted appearance and the forgotten stain of natural fruit jelly on her shirt. Her constant companion is her child, appropriately attired in politically correct T-shirts and little Birkenstock sandals.

3) Accoutrements

B) She is armed with all purpose massive shoulder bags filled with everything, she may possibly need: toys, babywipes, Heather Bishop tapes and a softball glove sticky with apple juice.

4) Habitat

D) Probably seen in a natural food store laden with kids—her bag of goodies and all her groceries and supplies piled into her net shopping bags—trying to pacify her screaming child.

5) Transportation

B) Her ideal form of transportation is a small station wagon or a practical hatchback that will accommodate her small arsenal of daily supplies: wagons, strollers, groceries and little playmates. More times than not her car has that lived-in appearance; its floor littered with all-natural Cheerios, toys and a long-forgotten pacifier.

6) Common Expressions

D) When in the presence of her child this lesbian is often heard saying, "Wipe your nose, or "Do you have to go to the bathroom now?" When among adults she talks about her kid—Only her kid.

7) Last Book Read

F) *The Butter Battle Book* by Dr. Seuss

8) Heroine

A) Dr. Penelope Leach, Child development specialist

9) Social Groups

A) Any meeting where politically correct daycare is provided.

Execudyke

Tank Suit (Corporate Membership at the Spa...)

Martini

Lord & Taylor Exec-U-Drag Suit jacket

Silk blouse & tie also seen at Nieman-Marcus

cut on dotted line to insert briefcase

Ring: to avoid awkward questions from straight colleagues

MONTH AT-A-GLANCE

Sack's Exec-U-Skirt

pantyhose in taupe, navy, smoke and "Blush"

Gucci pumps

107

1) Identification— C) Execudyke

2) Description

F) This Lesbian is readily identifiable in her execudrag—a slightly feminized version of the man's business suit. Her no-nonsense haircut is short enough to be out of her way, yet long enough to keep her from appearing radical. A few things give her away as a Lesbian—give a clue about what lurks behind this male-glorified exterior—the several empty holes in her ear lobes in addition to the two filled will gold and pearl studs, and the fact that the fingernails on her first two fingers of her right hand have been carefully shortened on an otherwise manicured hand.

3) Accoutrements

C) She is rarely seen without her briefcase which contains *The Wall Street Journal*, *Working Woman* magazine, calculator, Cross pen set and the ever important calendar book. For trips out of town she totes a lap top computer. At home she works on her terminal via the modem to her office, and her nationwide business network.

4) Habitat

A) This type of Lesbian can be found in meetings, in front of computer terminals, at airports and in restaurants having power lunches.

5)Transportation

C) A BMW, of course.

6) Common Expressions

A) "I have to work late." "I'm going to have to cancel." "Let's do lunch sometime." " I'll have my secretary call your secretary."

7) Last Book Read

E) Who has the time to read!

8) Heroine

D) Malcolm Forbes

9) Social Groups

B)She has a membership in Gay Professional Women but can't seem to fit the events into her busy schedule. Being too busy to date in person, she corresponds with other lesbians by writing letters to personals in gay computer bulletin boards.

PUZZLES WITH A MESSAGE

1 Things to do with Nancy Drew
1.   C A R S ON
2.   RIVER H EI G H T
3.   DET E CTIVE
4.   B L UE
5.   B O B
6.   MAR V IN
7.   NICK E RSON
8.   ROA D STER
9.   HANNAH G RUEN
10.   LAWY E R
11.   BL O ND
12.   C R OOKS
13.   FRI G HTENED
14.   N E XT CASE

2 What the process of going inward is
1.   ENCOUNTER G ROUPS
2.   PSYCHIC R EADINGS
3.   ISOLATION T ANKS
4.   AROMA T HERAPY
5.   PHYS I CAL THERAPY
6.   HYP N OSIS
7.   RE G RESSION
8.   HYDRO T HERAPY
9.   PSYCH O ANALYSIS
10.   TAL K RADIO
11.   ZE N
12.   ASTR O LOGY
13.   TALK SHOW S
14.   NU M EROLOGY
15.   SELF H E LPBOOKS

#3 Television Mothers Of The Past
1.   MOM P EEPERS
2.   GLORIA HEN R Y
3.   DONNA RE E D
4.   MARY T YLER MOORE
5.   JANE WYA T T
6.   ROSEMAR Y DECAMP
7.   BARBARA BILLI N GSLEY
8.   JE A N HAGEN
9.   DORIS D AY
10.   HO P E LANGE
11.   FLORENCE H E NDERSON
12.   MARION R OSS
13.   SYLVIA F IELD
14.   J EAN BYRON
15.   PEGGY C ASS
16.   HARRIE T NELSON

#4 How they acted
1.   GRETA G ARBO
2.   DOROTHY A R ZNER
3.   MAY W E ST
4.   HELEN HA Y YES
5.   MARLENE DEI T RICH
6. MERCEDES MCCAMB R IDGE
7.   JOAN CRAWF O RD
8.   TALLU L AH BANKHEAD
9.   KATHERINE H E PBURN
10.   INGRID BERG M AN
11.   MARY PICKF O RD
12.   BETTY D AVIS
13.   EVE ARD E N
14.   LILLIAN HEL L MAN
15.   LILLIAN GI S H

#5 MORE MOTHERS
ANN S O THERN
YVONNE D ECARLO
LIN D A LAVIN
JEAN ST A PLETON
NA N NCY WALKER
AUDREY MEA D OWS
ISABEL SAN F ORD
BEA ARTH U R
CAROLY N JONES
BONNIE FRAN K LIN
KA Y BALLARD

7 LESBIAN AUTHORS
1.   MC C ONNELL
2.   DREI S ER
3.   B A RR
4.   CH R ISTIAN
5.   WA L KER
6.   S C HULMAN
7.   FORRES T
8.   RUL E
9.   ALD R IDGE
10.   ALLI S ON

#6 BOOK STORES
1. SOUTHERN WILD S ISTERS UNLIMITED
2. OLD WIVES T ALES
3. BOOK GARD E N
4. FAUBOURGM A RIGNY BOOKS
5. HU M ANSPACE
6. THIRT Y FIRST STREET BOOKSTORE
7. LAMMA S WOMENS SHOP
8. BOOK P EOPLE
9. CATEGORY SI X BOOKS
10. LODÉ S TAR BOOKS
11. CARMI C HAELS
12. WOM E N AND CHILDREN FIRST
13. AMAZO N BOOKSTORE
14. EMMAS WOM E NS BOOKSTORE AND GIFTS
15. JUDITH S ROOM
16. MAL A PROPS BOOKS AND CAFE
17. NOW VOYAGE R
18. BEYOND TH E CLOSE T BOOKSTORE
19. NEWLEAF B OOKS
20. PANDORABOOK PE DDLARS
21. GERTRUDE S TEINMEMORIALBOOKSHOP
22. GOLDEN T HREADBOOKSELLERS
23. MAMA BEA R S CULTURE CENTER
24. FAN TH E FLAMES
25. DREAMS A ND SWORDS
26. LAMB D A PASSAGES
27. FULLC I RCLE BOOKS
28. COMMO N WOMAN BOOKS AND MORE
29. NEWWORDS B OOKSTORE
30. MOTH E R KALIS BOOKS
31. WOMANKIN D BOOKS

109

Solutions

"Quotables"

Simply unscramble each of the words horizontally to unearth a famous or infamous female quote. Here is an example. Solutions page...

Queen Victoria said,

"EW RAE ONT DMAUES"   ANSWER—We are not amused.

 # 1 Bette Midler said,

"I AM EVERYTHING YOU WERE AFRAID YOUR LITTLE GIRL WOULD GROW UP TO BE —AND YOUR LITTLE BOY.

 # 2 Elayne Boosier said,

"WOULDN'T IT BE GREAT IF YOU COULD ONLY GET AIDS FROM GIVING MONEY TO TELEVISION   PREACHERS ?"

 # 3 Muriel Spark in *The Prime of Miss Jean Brodie* said,

"GIVE ME A GIRL AT AN IMPRESSIONABLE AGE AND SHE IS MINE FOR LIFE."

 # 4 Robin Tyler, referring to Anita Bryant said,,

"ANITA, YOU ARE TO CHRISTIANITY WHAT PAINT-BY NUMBERS IS TO ART."

 # 5 Dolly Parton said,

"IT'S A GOOD THING THAT I WAS BORN A WOMAN, OR I'D HAVE BEEN A DRAG QUEEN."

Word Search 1

families

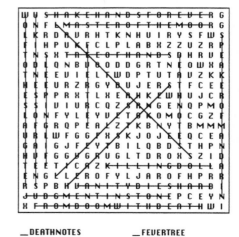

__BLENDED
__EXTENDED
__INTERRELIGIOUS
__TWOINCOME
__COMMUNAL
__FOSTER
__NUCLEAR

__DUALCAREER
__INTERETHNIC
__SINGLEPARENT
__EGALITARIAN
__INTERRACIAL
__SURROGATE

Ruth Rendell

__DEATHNOTES
__HEARTSTONES
__LAKEOFDARKNESS
__SHAKEHANDSFOREVER
__TREEOFHANDS
__WOLFTOTHESLAUGHTER
__FROMDOOMWITHDEATH
__KILLINGDOLL

__FEVERTREE
__JUDGMENTINSTONE
__LIVEFLESH
__SLEEPINGLIFE
__UNKINDNESSOFRAVENS
__MASTEROFTHEMOOR
__SPEAKEROFMANDARIN
__VANITYDIESHARD

110

Solutions

margaret atwood

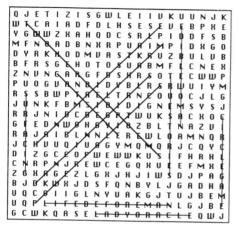

- BODILYHARM
- DANCINGGIRLS
- LIFEBEFOREMAN
- TWOHEADEDPOEMS
- CATSEYE
- EDIBLEWOMAN
- POWERPOLITICS
- CIRCLEGAME
- HANDMAIDSTALE
- SURFACING
- LADYORACLE
- TRUESTORIES

computers

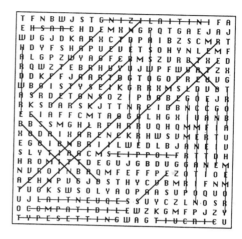

- ABORT
- CIRCUIT
- DATABASE
- DOCUMENTATION
- HARDWARE
- MEMORY
- PROGRAMMING
- TERMINAL
- BAUD
- COMPATIBILE
- DEBUGGING
- EDITING
- INITIALIZING
- MICROCOMPUTER
- SAVE
- TYPESETTING
- BOOTING
- CRASH
- DELETE
- ERROR
- INTERFACE
- OPERATING
- SEQUENTIAL
- BYTE
- CURSOR
- DISK
- FLOPPIES
- INTEGRATED
- PASSWORD
- SOFTWARE

marge piercy

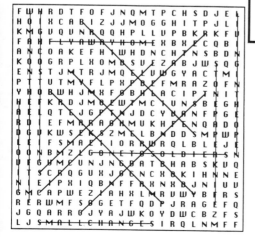

- BRAIDEDLIVES
- CIRCLESONTHEWATER
- GONETOSOLDIERS
- LIVINGINTHEOPEN
- STONEPAPERKNIFE
- WOMANONTHEEDGEOFTIME
- GOINGDOWNFAST
- HIGHCOSTOFLIVING
- SMALLCHANGES
- BREAKINGCAMP
- FLYAWAYHOME
- HARDLOVING
- MYMOTHERSBODY
- SUMMERPEOPLE

111

matching-fiction

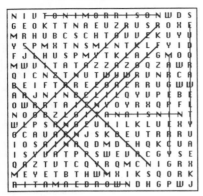

Book	Author
The Color Purple	Alice Walker
The Children of the Albatros	Anais Nin
Celestial Navigation	Anne Tyler
Jane and Prudence	Barbara Pym
As the Road Curves	Elizabeth Dean
Optimist's Daughter	Eudora Welty
Women of Brewster Place	Gloria Naylor
Vida	Marge Piercy
The Heart of a Woman	Maya Angelou
Sudden Death	Rita Mae Brown
Song of Solomon	Tony Morrison
To the Lighthouse	Virginia Wolf

ONLY ACTING

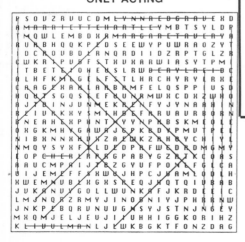

TV LADIES

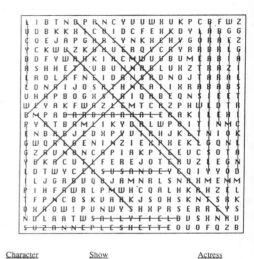

Character	Show	Actress
Jessica Fletcher	Murder She Wrote	Angela Lansbu
June Cleaver	Leave it to Beaver	Barbara Billing
Jeannie	I Dream of Jeannie	Barbara Eden
Della Street	Perry Mason	Barbara Hale
"Ma" Barkley	The Big Valley	Barbara Stanwy
Maude Findley	Maude	Bea Arthur
Colleen McMurphy	China Beach	Dana Delany
Julia Baker	Julia	Diahann Carroll
Julia Sugarbaker	Designing Women	Dixie Carter
Samantha Stevens	Bewitched	Elizabeth Montg
Marilyn McGrath	Heartbeat	Gail Strickland
Margaret Houlihan	M.A.S.H.	Loretta Switt
Lucy Ricardo	Lucy Ball	Lucie Ball
Anne Marie	That Girl	Marlo Thomas
Julie Barnes	MOD Squad	Peggy Lipton
Sally Rogers	The Dick Van 'Dyke' Show	Rosemarie
Sister Bertrille	The Flying Nun	Sally Field
Grace Van Owen	L.A. Law	Susan Dey
Emily Hartley	The Bob Newhart Show	Suzanne Pleshet
Rhoda Morgenstern	The Mary Tyler Moore Show	Valerie Harper

Movie	Actress
The Rose	Bette Midler
A Question of Love	Jane Alexander
Young Man and a Horn	Lauren Bacall
Desert Hearts (2)	Patricia Charvbonneau, Helen Sha
Silkwood	Cher
Personal Best (2)	Patrice Donnelly, Mariel Hemingw
The Color Purple (2)	Whoopi Goldberg, Margaret Avery
The Children's Hour (2)	Audrey Hepburn, Shirley MacLaine
Waiting for the Moon	Linda Hunt
The Killing of Sister George (2)	Beryl Reid, Susannah York
Manhattan	Meryl Streep
Persona	Liv Ulman
My Two Loves (2)	Lynn Redgrave, Mariette Hartley
Handmaid's Tale	Elizabeth McGovern

Solutions

Answers: DINNER PARTY

Answers: WATCH OUT BOYS

Answers: SIGNS

Answers: LITERARY WOMEN

Answers: FILM

Talk of the Town

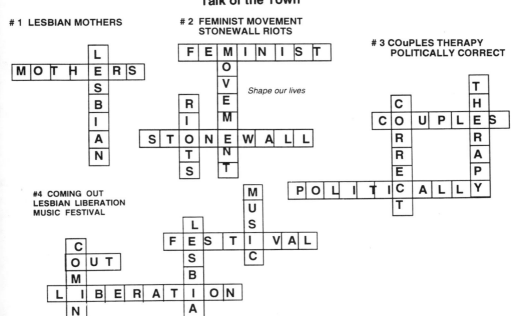

1 LESBIAN MOTHERS

2 FEMINIST MOVEMENT
STONEWALL RIOTS

Shape our lives

3 COUPLES THERAPY
POLITICALLY CORRECT

#4 COMING OUT
LESBIAN LIBERATION
MUSIC FESTIVAL

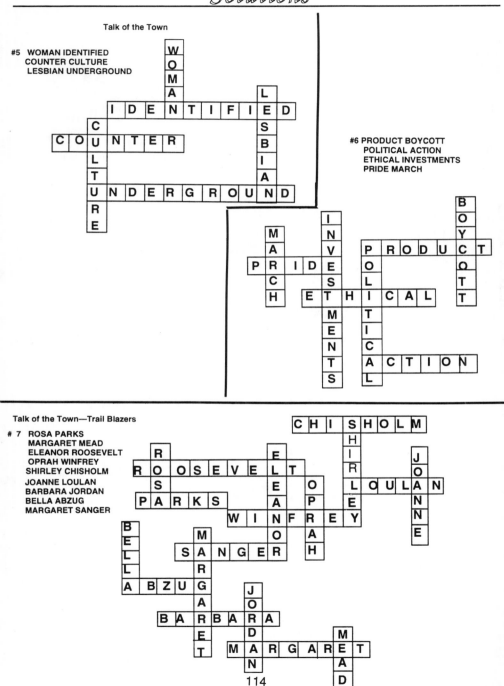

Talk of the Town

#5 WOMAN IDENTIFIED
COUNTER CULTURE
LESBIAN UNDERGROUND

#6 PRODUCT BOYCOTT
POLITICAL ACTION
ETHICAL INVESTMENTS
PRIDE MARCH

Talk of the Town—Trail Blazers

7 ROSA PARKS
MARGARET MEAD
ELEANOR ROOSEVELT
OPRAH WINFREY
SHIRLEY CHISHOLM
JOANNE LOULAN
BARBARA JORDAN
BELLA ABZUG
MARGARET SANGER

Solutions

MATCH-UP #1

UNDERSTANDING A THERAPIST'S LINGO
Select statements from the list below to match the appropriate therapist's statement.

What the therapist says...	What the therapist means...
How did that make you feel?	Let me hear all your inner hostility.
ow long have you been having these oughts?	I may have to refer her to a psychoanalist.
et's role play that situation.	Just how many personalities do you have?
s important for you to learn how to let go.	Chill out.
s fine to express your anger.	Yikes! She's certainly pissed off.
cuse me while I take this telephone call.	What price do you place on your sanity?
hank you for sharing.	Yippee! Another crisis!
ts discuss my fee.	Our time is up.

MATCH-UP #2

YOUR PARENTS AND YOUR LIFESTYLE
Select from the list of statements below to match the appropriate translation of the parental statement.

What your parents say...	What your parents mean...
would be nice if you dressed up this ristmas?	Could you wear something other than jeans and a t-shirt?
she coming home with you?	Are you still involved with a woman?
at hairstyle isn't my favorite.	You look like an army sergeant
ow many holes do you have in your r?	Heavens! What will your relatives think when they see better decorations on your ears than on our Christmas tree!
ve you ever met your cousin thur's best friend?	Why don't you give a man a try?
u two are welcome to sleep in the est room.	Twin beds will keep you apart!
hy don't you talk about the weather something else?	Whatever you do, don't mention the 'L' word.
e just want you to be happy.	We just want you to be straight.

MATCH-UP #3

YOU AND YOUR LOVER

at your lover says...	What your lover means...
e means never having to say 're sorry.	If you think I'm apologizing, you're wrong!
not afraid of a commitment.	I hope you're not suggesting we move in to-gether
hing happened with her.	I stopped myself just short of orgasm.
ybe we should spend some time rt.	Aren't twelve arguments in two hours a personal record for us?
's just a friend.	She wants to sleep with me.
eve me, there's no one else who erests me.	I haven't looked around in four days.
re are so many things about you t I love.	There are a million things you do that drive me nuts.
course what you do is important ne.	Tell me about your day after L.A. Law .
ve a headache.	Please be a love and bring me two aspirin, massage my neck for awhile, kiss my shoulders, lick my naked back, and then make wild, passionate love to me for hours.

MATCH-UP #4

BAR PICK-UP LINES
from the list of statements below to match the appropriate translation of the pick-up line.

What you hear...	What it means...
ne here often?	My lover and I just split up and I haven't seen the inside of a bar for the past five years.
n't usually ask anyone to ce.	I haven't been able to figure out what to do on the dance floor since disco died.
what do you do for work?	Are you rich?
those your friends you're ?	Is the diesel dyke with the knife in her back pocket your lover?
n I buy you a drink?	I guess I'll hang out with you until I get bored.
wded, isn't it?	I can't stop rubbing my body against yours.
e that shirt.	God, you have great cleavage.
're a really fascinating lady.	I have a half hour 'til last call to try to score with you.
really like to get to know you.	Let's sleep together.

MATCH-UP #5

NANCY DREW MYSTERY STORIES
Here's Nancy Drew again. One of the few strong women models from our childhood. Use the list of clues and the story titles listed below to match the published title of the Nancy Drew mystery to its appropriate clue.

Clues	The story title
Hush-hush, antique tick-tick	The Secret of the Old Clock
Info in busted jewelry	The Clue of the Broken Locket
Info in ancient pictures	The Clue in the Old Album
Termite-phobic hush-hush woman	The Secret of the Wooden Lady
Dorothy's puzzling footwear	The Scarlet Slipper Mystery
Can't find the pane puzzle	The Hidden Window Mystery
Info from crooked smoker	The Clue of the Leaning Chimney
Look for lost directions	The Quest of the Missing Map
Puzzle at house of plants	The Mystery at the Moss-Covered Mansion
Airborn Rossinols puzzle	The Mystery at the Ski Jump
Empty tree note	The Message in the Hollow Oak
The meaning of weird wax	The Sign of the Twisted Candles
Me and my out west hush-hush	The Secret at Shadow Ranch
Circular circus hush-hush	The Ringmaster's Secret
Ebony unlockers info	The Clue of the Black Keys
Spectre in Blackwood corridor	The Ghost of Blackwood Hall
Hush-hush under the elderly roof	The Secret in the Old Attic
Info in precious metals container	The Clue in the Jewel Box
Puzzle of the metal bonded elephant's nose	The Mystery of the Brass Bound Trunk
Info in journal	The Clue in the Diary

MATCH-UP #8

#1 LESBIAN ANNIVERSARY GIFTS
Select items from the list of Lesbian Gifts below to match the appropriate anniversary year.

Year	Traditional Gift	Lesbian Gift
1st	Paper	Subscription to a gay newspaper
2nd	Cotton	T-shirt from the Michigan Women's Festival
3rd	Leather	Leather dildo harness
4th	Fruit, flowers	Passion fruit and ladyslippers
5th	Wood	A cord of split wood
6th	Candy	Tofu chocolate
7th	Wool, copper	L.L. Bean shirt, plaid,
8th	Bronze	Gift certificate to a tanning salon
9th	Pottery	Statue of a Greek goddess
10th	Tin	Earth-conscious paper bags to store recyclable tin cans
11th	Steel	Black and Decker Skil Saw
12th	Silk	Lavendar silk sheets
13th	Lace	Rawhide shoe laces for work boots
14th	Ivory	A case of heavy-duty hand cleaner
15th	Crystal	A psychically in-tune quartz
20th	China	A take-out Chinese dinner
25th	Silver	A pair of silver earrings in the shape of handcuffs
30th	Pearl	A copy of Audubon's Guide to Seashells
35th	Coral	Scuba diving equipment
40th	Ruby	An original recording by Ruby and the Romantics
45th	Sapphire	An encyclopedia of precious stones and gems
50th	Gold	An autographed copy of Tracy Chapman's first gold album
55th	Emerald	A Wizard of Oz video
60th	Diamond	Purchase of a softball field
75th	Diamond	Dedication of the softball field

115

Solutions

MATCH-UP #6

SOFTBALL ATHLETES' EXCUSES
Select from the list of statements below to match the appropriate softball excuse.

What they say...

The umping stank.

Their clean up batter takes steroids.

I can't stand their pitcher.

I had a good hit in the third inning.

Their playing field is a mess.

The people watching the game were really loud and obnoxious.

What they mean...

We sucked.

Our cleanup batter can't hit out of the in-field.

Their pitcher is my ex.

I was one for six at the plate.

If they hadn't spent two hours lining the damn field, the fair ball wouldn't have been so obvious...

At least they had fans...

MATCH-UP #7

STATEMENTS FROM THE POLITICALLY INCORRECT
Select from the list of statements below to match the appropriate political sentiment.

What they say...

I really care what happens to dolphins.

I'm cutting down on meat.

Abused women need help.

I recycle.

Animals have rights too.

It's important to support lesbian businesses.

I support lesbian politicians.

What they mean...

I won't do my imitation of Flipper again.

I only eat two burgers instead of three.

Tomorrow I'm asking my boss for a raise.

I redeem my empties.

I slow down every time I see a squirrel crossing the road.

I drop ten bucks every Saturday night at the bar.

If she's cute, I'll vote for her.

Building Blocks #1 SayWhat?

Solution page...

```
R O V E R B A L O L Y O N L Y
D E A R N H E A R I N G I N G
I M O N S I G N S V R E S T R
A L H E I R O G L Y P H S S I
D N T C O M M U N I C A T E E
H A I L A B R A I L L E D E R
N U N V R B L G E S T U R E S
V E R C O N V E R S A T I O N
```

Building Blocks #2 Praise Be

Solution page...

```
O G O D D E S S I N H I S E
A L I N A S P R A Y E R O H
S T I K A W I C C A D A Y R
I W A N T A R O T C A K K E
M Y S T I C I S M Y S C E T
M E D I T A T I O N A T O N
A N T N A T U R E C A L S U
V C T V C H A N N E L I N G
R E W O R E L I G I O N L Y
M A S C E T I C I S M Y S T
A S S A I N T S C O M A R C
H I R H O L Y Y R O L Y N G
```

Building Blocks #3 Let's Talk

Solution page...

```
O U B L O O P E O C O U P L E S E T
L U F A K E C O N O M I C O M I C O
G R O W L O G R O U P I N L Y G R E
O C C U P A T I O N A L N A T A N C
T E X C E P R E X S E X Y U A L L M
H A R D A R C A R E E R C L F E A V
P O O H S C H O O L S O S H A L P T
M O D A M R F A M I L Y D I S F N J
I N C I D E I N I N D I V I D U A L
W H I M A R R I A G E A V E R G O W
```

Building Blocks #4 Don'tAssume

Solution page...

```
B L O C L A S S I S M L E S E
F A K B E A U T Y I S K I M D
W I T I D I V E R S I T Y G R
C V D I F F E R E N C E S A N
X C E G E N D E R I N R A L L
R D A R C A R O L E S P L A A
O H O R O F S T I G M A S L P
M A J O R I T Y L Y Y U L E S
C I D E S T E P M O T H E R S
I M A S T R A I G H T S U G O
M S T X S T N N A M E S H R T
S N U M E R A G E I S M M L Y
```

Building Blocks #5 Women's Work cont.

Solution page...

```
N T U N A G E I S H A S G R L S
P E E N S T E N O G R A P H E R
G H O T E L R T E L L E R T E R
K B O O K K E E P E R S P E R A
C I D E A G E N T S N U T T S N
A M A S S E U S E S U E S S E S
P O P R O S T I T U T E S E D Y
C C A R E G I V E R S A N T K R
C R E A R E C E P T I O N I S T
```

Building Blocks #5 Women's Work Cont.

Solution page...

```
G O O C S O C O O K S P O O S K
M E D I E D U C A T O R S T A L
R E C R E S E C R E T A R I E S
N U M U V O L U N T E E R S T Y
A L S T R I P P E R S O M A L S
N O H O M E M A K E R S I N L Y
U N N U T R I T I O N I S T E D
Y P P S Y C H I C S M Y S M T Y
C O U N S E L O R S I M D H L P
S T R U N N U N S B U L M D U L
P E R E S T E S E E R S R E E R
```

```
N U M R O N O F I R S T L A D Y
E R K C E C L E R K S K E A E R
O L E D O L I M O D E L S L A M
D I E T I C I A N S N A T A N S
L I B R A T E L I B R A R I A N
E R A H I N H E A L E R S E A R
```

116

2

Since we met last time...

Authors' Biographies

Elizabeth Dean is still trying to sort out who Amy Dean is, who was also credited with writing the original *Cut-Outs and Cut-Ups*. After a year of intensive therapy to separate the two personalities, she's waiting nervously to see who will also be credited with writing this new book.

Linda Wells is an aspiring librarian (dare to dream!) who spent her entire fortune from royalty checks on a giddy spending spree at every yard sale, flea market and Unitarian Church auction in Massachusetts.

Andrea Curran has been basking in the wealth accrued from the royalties from her last book, *Cut-Outs and Cut-Ups*, by swimming in the neighbors' pool, riding her twenty-year old ten-speed bike, and splurging on small Heath Bar Crunch cones at the local ice cream stand. She has also become an adept interpreter for the humor impaired (or is that humorously challenged?), spending a great deal of time explaining the nuances of various humorous situations to people who couldn't care less.

Other Books from New Victoria

Mystery-Adventure

She Died Twice — Jessica Lauren—The remains of a child are unearthed and Emma is forced to relive the weeks leading up to Natalie's death as she searches for the murderer. ISBN 0-9-34678-34-0 ($8.95)

Woman with Red Hair—Brunel—The mystery of her mother's death takes Magalie into the swamps and the slums of France, her only clue the memory of a woman with red hair. ISBN 0-934678-30-8 ($8.95)

Death by the Riverside—Redmann—Detective Mickey Knight finds herself slugging through thugs and slogging through swamps to expose a dangerous drug ring. ISBN 0-934678-27-8 ($8.95)

Mysteries by Sarah Dreher

A Captive In Time—Stoner finds herself inexplicably transported to a small town in the Colorado Territory, time 1871. When, if ever, will she find a phone to call home? ISBN 0-934678-22-7 ($9.95)

Stoner McTavish — The first Stoner mystery—Dream lover Gwen, in danger in the Grand Tetons. *"Sensitive, funny and unabashedly sweet, Stoner McTavish is worth the read."* ($7.95) ISBN 0-934678-06-5

Something Shady— Stoner gets trapped in the clutches of the evil Dr. Millicent Tunes. *"The piece de resistance of the season...I think it's the funniest book I ever read."* ($8.95) ISBN 0-934678-07-3

Gray Magic— Stoner and Gwen head to Arizona, but a peaceful vacation turns frightening when Stoner becomes a combatant in the great struggle between the Hopi Spirits of good and evil. ($8.95) ISBN-0-934678-11-1

Adventure / Romance

Shadows of Aggar— Chris Anne Wolfe — Amazon, Diana, born into a woman-only society is an undercover agent on a medieval planet. There she and Shadow guide, Elana.attempt to prevent all-out intergalactic war. ($9.95) ISBN 0-934678-36-7

Touch of Music— Dorothy Clarke—Roxanna and Becky are part of a lesbian household .Conflict plagues their relationship until Roxanna's daughter is hospitalized, and they find that their differences are not so important after all. ($8.95) ISBN 0-934678-31-6

Kite Maker— Van Auken—Melvina drives up to a women's bar in a spiffy new Cadillac convertible...and drives off with Sal , one of the mainstays of the community, in search of a long lost friend. ($8.95) ISBN 0-934678-32-4

Cody Angel—Whitfield—Dana looks for self-esteem and love through emotional entanglements—with her boss, with Frankie, a bike dyke, and Jerri, who enjoys sex as power. ISBN 0-934678-28-6 ($8.95)

In Unlikely Places—Beguin—Following a dream of exploring Africa, nineteenth century adventurer Lily Bascombe finds herself searching for the elusive Miss Margery Pool. ISBN 0-934578- 25-1 ($8.95)

Mari — Hilderley.—The story of the evolving relationship between Mari, an Argentinian political activist, and Judith, a New York City musician. ISBN-0-934678- 23-5 ($8.95)

Dark Horse— Lucas—Fed up with corruption in local politics, lesbian Sidney Garrett runs for mayor falling in love with a socialite campaign worker. ISBN-0-934678--21-9 ($8.95)

As The Road Curves—Dean—Ramsey, with a reputation for never having to sleep alone, takes off from a prestigious lesbian magazine on an adventure of a lifetime. ISBN 0-934678-17-0 ($8.95)

All Out—Alguire—Winning at the Olympics is Kay's all-consuming goal until a romance threatens her ability to go all out for the gold. ISBN-0-934678-16-2 ($8.95)

Look Under the Hawthorn—Frye—Stonedyke Edie Cafferty from Vermont searches for her long lost daughter and meets Anabelle, a jazz pianist looking for her birth mother. ISBN-0-934678-12-X ($7.95)

Runway at Eland Springs— Béguin—Flying supplies into the African bush, Anna gets herself into conflict with a game hunter, and finds love and support with Jilu, the woman at Eland Springs. ISBN-0-934678-10-3 ($7.95).

Promise of the Rose Stone—McKay—Mountain warrior Issa is banished to the women's compound in the living satellite where she and her lover Cleothe plan an escape with Cleothe's newborn baby. ISBN-0-934678-09-X ($7.95)

Humor

Cut Outs and Cut Ups (1) A Fun'n Games Book for Lesbians—Dean, Wells, and Curran—Games, puzzles, astrology, paper dolls—an activity book for lesbians . ISBN-0-934678-20-0 ($8.95)

Found Goddesses: Asphalta to Viscera—Grey & Penelope—"*Found Goddesses is wonderful. I've had more fun reading it than any book in the last two years.*"—Joanna Russ. ISBN-0-934678-18-9 ($7.95)

Morgan Calabresé; The Movie—N. Dunlap- Wonderfully funny comic strips. Politics, relationships, and softball as seen through the eyes of Morgan Calabresé ISBN-0-934678-14-6 ($5.95)

Short Fiction/Plays

Secrets—Newman—The surfaces and secrets, the joys and sensuality and the conflicts of lesbian relationships are brought to life in these stories. ISBN 0-934678-24-3 ($8.95)

Lesbian Stages—"Sarah Dreher's plays are good yarns firmly centered in a Lesbian perspective with specific, complex, often contradictory (just like real people) characters." — Kate McDermott ($ 9.95) ISBN 0-934678-15-4

The Names of the Moons of Mars— Schwartz—In these stories the author writes humorously as well as poignantly about our lives as women and as lesbians. ISBN-0-934678-19-7 ($8.95)
Audiotape read by author ($9.95) ISBN 0-934678-26-X

Available from your favorite bookstore or
Order directly from New Victoria Publishers, PO Box 27 Norwich, Vt. 05055